NOT JUST A PRETTY PLACE
SURVIVAL IN SNOWDONIA

Not Just a Pretty Place
Survival in Snowdonia

Huw Jenkins

First published in 2009

© Huw Jenkins

© Llygad Gwalch 2009

ISBN: 978-1-84524-151-3

Cover design: Carreg Gwalch

Published by Llygad Gwalch,
12 Iard yr Orsaf, Llanrwst, Wales LL26 0EH
tel: 01492 624031
fax: 01492 641502
email: books@carreg-gwalch.com
website: www.carreg-gwalch.com

To the long term survival
of this wonderful part of the world

Contents

Foreword

Iolo Williams

Snowdonia is a magical land of myths, legends, magnificent scenery and stunning wildlife. This book celebrates the survival of wildlife, including man himself, in this rugged part of north-western Wales and highlights issues, big and small, that affect each and every one of us.

The stories link landscape, people and wildlife into an optimistic view of the future with subjects as diverse as the rare and elusive pine marten, freshwater pearl mussels and local foods. Underneath the humour and optimism, however, there are serious messages about the viability of our lifestyles. Why is the pine marten, once our second commonest carnivore, now so rare? Why do we continue to import food from the far ends of the earth when we have so much excellent local produce? These are all questions that deserve an answer.

If someone read this book in a thousand years' time, they would probably conclude that people and wildlife co-habited relatively harmoniously in Snowdonia at the beginning of the 21st century. Wouldn't it be wonderful if they also said that it was around this time that we significantly changed our approach to our environment and sustainable living.

Introduction

New people are infuriating: they are forever telling you about their new-found discoveries, about things that have been around for ages. I'm one of those people, new to Snowdonia (in Welsh, *Eryri*) a few years ago, and loving every moment of it. It's got a dreamlike quality that's familiar, which might be down to childhood day trips from our home in central Wales, or maybe to the Rupert Bear books being illustrated by a man who lived in Beddgelert.

Shortly after arriving I attended an event called 'A Walk on the Wildside', aimed to inspire local people to make more of what is around us in attracting visitors to the area. Our guide was Twm Elias, from Plas Tan y Bwlch, the national park's training centre, and he started off .... 'It's not just a pretty landscape, you know…' I was so impressed with what followed, the stories and history he told, that I wrote up the event for the benefit of those who couldn't attend.

Since that day I have been unable to stop exploring, talking and writing about the wonderful things that lie just below the surface of this 'pretty landscape'.

In my pursuit of knowledge I've become an obsessive training course participant – every time I see an event publicised I juggle my diary and book myself on. I can't help myself, and when I get back I convert my findings and photos into a short story, and many of these get posted on the local BBC website.

I bombarded the 'Beeb' with so many of these stories they decided to give me

Nantlle Ridge with Yr Wyddfa in the distance

a microphone and basic training to be one of Radio Wales' community reporters, seeking out and recording local stories with interest for listeners across Wales, generally quirky and with happy endings. There is no shortage of material in Snowdonia.

Due to the mountainous nature of the land, the low density population and national park status, there has been minimal development to wipe away the past. It's like walking through a slice of evolution. Over the years some things have fallen by the wayside: creatures such as the beavers didn't make it. They were too tasty, and by the thirteenth century had been hunted to extinction. But the habitat is still right for them and very soon I expect they will be reintroduced in line with the rest of Europe.

The really great news is that so many other things have survived. Some of the plants are thriving, such as the lichens and bryophytes, whilst others cling on to a delicate balance such as the arctic alpines on the north facing slopes of the highest mountains. Wild mountain goats are multiplying, sometimes at the expense of people's gardens and the next generation of oak trees. Pine martens are about, but can we prove it?

It's not just things you can see and touch but the intangibles such as language, tradition and a spirit of community that have survived. Not tucked away in a book or museum but out there in everyday life.

The trouble is that many things are 'just clinging on' and, unless we re-think the way we go about our lives, they won't be here for ever.

Most of our salt marsh lamb ends up in France and our lobsters in Spain whilst we eat lamb from New Zealand and prawns from Thailand – talk about food miles! Over 90 percent of charcoal used on our barbecues is imported and, as if that wasn't bad enough, much of it comes from unsustainable sources such as mangrove forests in Indonesia. Meanwhile local charcoal from hardwood, made as a by-product of Welsh woodland management, is not only eco-friendly but far higher quality – we should insist on it and help breathe life back into the rural economy.

I've always been a person who sees things as half full as opposed to half empty. It's not all doom and gloom: there is a tide of opinion gathering momentum and some really positive things happening – I just wish they would happen a bit faster.

This collection of stories aims to give a flavour of what is around when we spend time in Snowdonia, so much more than a pretty landscape.

Mwynhewch! (enjoy!)

Huw Jenkins, May 2009

On Foot

Modern transport tends to whisk you along too fast to appreciate your surroundings and most of the roads are low down. By contrast the ancient trackways of Snowdonia rise up from the valleys and coast to traverse the high ground, through rocky or boggy terrain unsuitable for today's agricultural land 'improvement'. Apart from the occasional reservoir or conifer plantation these old routes are untouched, and travelling here is like walking through a living museum rich in reminders of the way we lived.

We can walk past the standing stones of Bronze Age routes or where Roman legionnaires marched or bone-shaking coaches carried passengers to and from ships to Ireland; journeying where drovers ushered their livestock hundreds of miles to market or smugglers evaded taxes on salt or brandy; following in the footsteps of pilgrims, miners and shepherds. Up here our past is highly visible and preserved.

'On foot' is the sensual way to experience Snowdonia, with lungs, stretched by the gradients, breathing in pure Atlantic air or the scents of gorse and bog myrtle, boots squidging through bogs or grating on Cambrian rock, whilst feral goats note your presence and buzzards cry.

All is well apart from the scourge of the occasional joy-rider on a 4x4 or trails bike, churning up the ground, and RAF jets breaking the spell.

Coast to coast through the heart of Snowdonia

From the north coast at Conwy to the west coast at Harlech this fifty mile walk through the heart of Snowdonia is rich in history that can be seen and touched, and links places across mountains that are miles apart by car.

Just a few minutes up the North Wales Path, with blooming heather and wild ponies pressing through the tall bracken, suburbia seems far away. Looking back to Conwy the castle looks in perfect condition despite seven centuries of wear and tear. For a while it was captured and held by Owain Glyndŵr's men who gained entrance dressed as women and slaughtered the guard. They say the river ran red for many days – history through rose-tinted specs depending which side you were on.

As you emerge from the footpath at the top of the Sychnant Pass, Puffin Island comes into view just off the coast of Anglesey. Brown rats landed here in 1890 and severely threatened the birds, but the Countryside Council for Wales have now eliminated the rats. The surviving puffins can once again flourish on their namesake island, which is also home to 36 per cent of the cormorants in Wales.

Further along is the Sychnant Pass Stone Circle. One of the largest stones has been blasted apart and you can see the drill marks into which the explosive was stuffed. Presumably this act of destruction was in response to high chapel incitement against paganism as opposed to hooliganism.

The Iron Age hill forts of Caer Bach and Pen-y-Gaer look down into the Conwy valley where the Romans built their fort near the river. There is an air of military confidence in the Roman choice of site, out in the open without the natural defences of a mountain top, but with the ability to supply and reinforce by boat.

Beneath and to the west of Pen-y-Gaer there is a long leat built to divert rainwater into a series of inter-connected reservoirs, including Llyn Eigiau. The beautiful upland valley is scarred by the odd-looking, L-shaped dam wall, about three-quarters of a mile long. Following torrential rain in 1925, twenty-six inches in five days, the inadequate foundations were washed away and the dam was breached. The torrent swept away the dam below and crashed down the mountain onto Dolgarrog, killing sixteen people. Many more would have perished were it not for the film being shown at the village hall whilst the church was swept away with its bell tolling.

One of the connected reservoirs is Llyn Cowlyd, supplying water to Llandudno and the hydro-electric plant for the old aluminium works. With a depth of 229 feet it is the deepest lake in northern Wales, a natural lake extended by a wall 45 feet

Bryn Cader Faner on the Bronze Age trackway from Harlech to Trawsfynydd

high. The slopes of the surrounding mountains plunge so steeply that the area has not been forested for hundreds of years.

Crossing the A5 at Capel Curig the route goes around the east side of Moel Siabod along Sarn Offeiriaid (*'the priest's path'*). Sticking out above the trees is Dolwyddelan Castle, built by the Welsh in the early thirteenth century – it must have held a formidable grip over the flow of people between Meirionnydd and Conwy. The name Dolwyddelan (*'meadow of the Irishman'*) is derived from the Celtic missionary St Gwyddelan, who came here to help reinforce the Christian message.

A steep climb onto the moorland and along disused tramways through Victorian slate workings, until you reach Manod Quarry, the bomb-proof home to the National Gallery when it was evacuated here during the Second World War.

The route follows Sarn Helen, the Roman road connecting forts in northern Wales. 'Sarn' means causeway and Helen is derived from 'lleng', the Welsh word for legion. This is one of the best-preserved stretches of upland Roman roads in Britain. It looks pretty worn out and run down, but after 1900 years of rain, sheep and floods it's an achievement that it survived at all.

A short deviation from the track is Bryn y Castell, an Iron Age fort where iron

13

was smelted from bog ore. There's a bog below, but the trees for charcoal and smelting are long gone.

At the corner of the Welsh Water building a reproduction engraved stone from the fifth century announces *'Cantiorix Hic iacit, Venedotis cives fuit, consobrinos Magli magistrat'* – 'Cantiorix lies here. He was a citizen of Gwynedd and a cousin of Maglos the magistrate.' Venedotia is the old Latin name for the territory of Gwynedd.

Towards the golf course above Llan Ffestiniog is an area known as Beddau Gwŷr Ardudwy, the 'graves of the Ardudwy Men'. The story goes that the men of Ardudwy were short of brides so they stole the women from Clwyd. Somewhat peeved, the men of Clwyd attacked and killed the Ardudwy men. Instead of rejoicing, the rescued women drowned themselves in the nearby Llyn Morwynion (*'the maidens' lake'*).

Across the Cynfal and up through the forestry you rejoin the Roman road to Tomen y Mur with its small amphitheatre. It is unusual to have an amphitheatre at an auxiliary fort (auxiliaries being non-Romans), supporting the theory that this was a training fort, a place of instruction as opposed to one of enjoyment.

Not far from here a wooden book was discovered made from thin sheets of wood hollowed out for a rectangular patch of beeswax. A stylus was used to form characters by scratching away the beeswax to reveal the wood beneath. It turns out to be part of a will and is one of only five Roman wills in the world – the other four were all found in Egypt.

The route continues over the long footbridge on stilts at the shallow end of Llyn Trawsfynydd. The first dam was built in the 1920s to feed the hydro-electric scheme near Maentwrog, which began generating in 1928.

Dam walls were extended in the 1960s to provide water for cooling the nuclear reactors, which used 35 million gallons per hour. Stone and concrete piers were constructed to aid the circulation and cooling of the water, a bit like a radiator. Rumour has it that fish used to grow very big in these steamy waters.

This was the UK's first and only inland nuclear power station. Ironically plans for its construction were approved in 1955, just four years after the area was declared a national park.

On the far side of the lake the route rises upwards on the Bronze Age trackway that emerges from under the water. The track winds around the side of the mountain to Bryn Cader Faner, a magnificent circle of standing stones sometimes referred to as the Welsh Crown of Thorns. The circle is easily seen from the west, but hidden just below the brow when coming from Trawsfynydd. The stones have been rearranged from their original positions – a consequence of grenade practice in the Second World War!

I walked past more standing stones, hut circles and burial cairns then steeply down the mountain to the beach and felt the welcome relief of sand between my toes. Edward's castle at Conwy is a few days march away but his Harlech bastion is looming on the skyline above. Closing my eyes to reflect on what I have seen between these 700 year old relics of English oppression – masses of visible history that has endured the test of time, not to mention the culture and spirit of a fiercely independent people. What I have seen is so fantastic it would be easy to think it was a dream – but it's all for real.

Barmouth without the tack

Driving west off the M6 onto the M54 and relative tranquility, my grip on the steering wheel relaxes a bit. By-passing leafy Shrewsbury and on through Welshpool, the world is beginning to look magical. Hills become mountains, hedges turn to stone walls and streams to waterfalls. In front of Cadair Idris the road drops steeply to Dolgellau, a fairy-tale market town of listed buildings, and onwards along the Mawddach estuary. Scenery and superlatives build to a crescendo ... until I turn the corner at Barmouth.

Kiss-Me-Quick seaside tack hits me in the face, and this shock is reinforced as I try to escape up the coast through miles of caravan parks, so much metal and plastic amongst the ancient rocks and seascape.

But since that first visit I've mellowed and matured, and know a much better way to approach and appreciate Barmouth. That beautiful scenic road along the edge of the estuary is relatively new, not being opened until 1798. If you like walking, the old road is even better and like many of the ancient trackways is built high up in the hills. In olden times building roads along rivers and coastline was a waste of effort as the water provided a ready-made surface.

From above Bontddu you can walk a well preserved section of the old coach road from London to Harlech. At one point there's a fork in the road with a milestone, offering you a 10-mile route to Harlech or a 5-mile route to Tal-y-bont. I took the Tal-y-bont turn and thence a spur off to Barmouth. In places these old tracks are gouged through great hunks of rock and surprisingly narrow, the coaches must have been skinny to get through, with just enough room for two horses abreast. Also, the routes are very steep, and you can imagine people having to get out and walk, or even push on occasion.

This trackway took me on to Barmouth and when I say 'on', I mean 'on top of'. Clinging precariously to the cliffs are some wonderful old buildings approached by steep and twisty little lanes that should by rights be cobbled. You are so close to windows and doors it's impossible not to be nosy. This part of town is called The Rock, as in Gibraltar.

Above The Rock is The Frenchman's Grave. Auguste Guyard was an educationalist and philosopher exiled from France, who shared similar beliefs to the likes of John Ruskin: that there should be social justice such as housing and education for the underprivileged. Guyard was renowned for his gardening skills and knowledge of medicinal plants, and these terraced gardens might have been tended or inspired by him.

He was a tenant of Fanny Talbot, who did many good works for the locals and

Bottlenose dolphins overlooking the harbour

provided several cottages for use by impoverished people. These were known as the Ruskin Cottages. Fanny is also famous for being the first person ever to donate land to the National Trust. She gave the 5 acre stretch of land above The Rock, called Dinas Oleu (*'fortress of light'*), so that its spectacular views could be enjoyed in perpetuity by all.

From this vantage point there's a great view of the harbour. Ships have been sailing in and out of Barmouth for centuries, and there is a record from 1587 of Le Angell de Bermo carrying rye and barley to St David's.

Between 1770 and 1800 there were 147 ships built along the Mawddach. The catalyst for this surge in ship-building was the combination of a booming woollen-cloth industry, and the collapse of the monopoly of the Shrewsbury Guild of Drapers. For hundreds of years the Guild, established by Royal Charter, had acted as the middleman or mafia of the trade. Most Welsh produce was sold at market in Oswestry and taken by heavily-armed members of the Guild for finishing off in Shrewsbury and thence by packhorse train to London and onward export.

Barmouth became the staging depot for woollen products made in Dolgellau and used to clothe slaves on plantations and as uniforms for the armies of Catherine the Great.

One alleged source of the name Barmouth is that merchants and sailors created it as being easy enough for the non-Welsh to use. Seems a bit far-fetched (although I would believe a similar proposition being necessary for Machynlleth!). The Welsh name is Abermaw, meaning mouth of the Mawddach, and the colloquial version of Bermo is made up of the middle letters.

Looking down on the town there are many chapels and churches to be seen, chapels for the working class Welsh and churches for the gentry and English. St John's church was built in 1889 and funded by the Perrins family, of Lea & Perrins fame, who had a lavish holiday home in the town.

At the bottom of The Rock and across the main road is a haunting statue in marble carved by the internationally famous local sculptor, Frank Cocksey, to celebrate the millennium. The marble is one of the forty-three blocks thought to be quarried from Carrara in northern Italy and lost in 1709 when a Genoese galleon was shipwrecked on Sarn Badrig, off the coast from Tal-y-bont. One theory is that the ship was off course on its way to London delivering marble for a prestigious building. If you look at either end of the statue you can see the effects of 'marine borers' chewing away at the marble for three hundred years, gouging out little caves for their shells.

Sarn Badrig is a reef or causeway, which runs twelve miles out to sea and was formed by boulders being piled up as the glaciers slipped off Snowdonia at the end of the last Ice Age. It's a bit of a hazard to shipping, but great for the local diving club and a hot spot for sea anglers.

At the end of a walk like this it's good to sit and reflect at a harbourside café, enjoy a cool drink on a hot summer's day, and soak up the view. With Cadair Idris as the backdrop, a steam train crossing the bridge over the estuary, its arches reflected in the still waters, and a seal begging fish from the incoming boats, what more could one wish for?

At this point it's best to sail off into the sunset, with romantic memories untarnished by seaside tack.

Ras fynydd

Ras y Moelwyn is an arduous fell run from Blaenau Ffestiniog over the three peaks of Moelwyn Mawr, Moelwyn Bach and Moel yr Hydd. Ten and a half miles, many ups and downs and relics galore of the slate industry.

I'd always aspired to do a fell run, but to do one on my doorstep was especially appealing. The term 'fell running' sounds a bit too much like the Yorkshire Dales – 'ras fynydd' or 'mountain racing' is much more appropriate to this country and its geography.

At registration I can see this is going to be no leisurely stroll. The atmosphere is competitive, albeit friendly. The plastic water bottle in my hand looks very amateurish and out of place with the purpose-built bum bags and knapsacks. One of the experienced runners tells me to leave it behind, 'Drink lots before the race and don't forget to go to the loo.'

As the starting time approached there was much running up and down the field: they must have overdosed on high-energy food. Entrants were exchanging comments about recent runs in distant parts of Britain. About 120 of us gathered around the starting funnel. There was no gun, no 'ready steady go', just a nod from the official and without any elbowing the party rolled into action, some a bit faster than others.

I was hardly in pole position at the start and set off with a conservative (as in conserving energy) stride. It was great to catch up with the rest as we bunched up to squeeze through narrow gates and stiles. But pretty soon it was open countryside and the real talent was rushing to the horizon. By the time I got to Cwm Cwmorthin the leaders were on their way out.

'That's nothing to worry about,' I told myself, 'focus on the moment not the end. This is an exercise in free will, I'll run to the next rock and then make a decision whether to go on.' In bite-size chunks, the prospect of what lay ahead was not so awesome.

There was plenty to look at to take my mind off the race. Millions of tons of slate arranged in tiers cascading down to Llyn Cwmorthin with the windows of the quarrymen's ruined barracks watching on. Poking out from the path were sections of old tramways and set in the middle of the Cwm an impressive but derelict chapel. Rising out from the far end was the trackway down which finished slate was once brought by packhorse.

I managed to run up the first section in short strides, but as the gradient grew steeper I relented to a dogged walk. Upwards, beyond more quarries, funicular inclines and workshops, it's surprising how many people you can overtake with a dogged walk. I thought I was doing well until I pointed downhill from the top of Moelwyn Mawr. Bounding down the mountain in great leaps and strides the 'winged' feet of experienced runners I'd overtaken came whistling past me. No point wasting energy slogging uphill, they'd saved it and used their skill and experience to fly down the mountain, picking out safe footing on the most precarious of slopes.

A windswept huddle of cheery marshalls were at the bwlch (pass) between the mountains to count and cheer us on – 'Da iawn, daliwch ati!' Battling to the top of Moelwyn Bach, feeling that 'bach' might mean something other than 'small', I circled the cairn and launched into the descent. There are moments of sheer fear and of delight as you break off from a piece of the cliff and sprint into a spongy peat bog. At last a stretch of flat even ground as we ran across the dam wall of Stwlan, part of Britain's first pumped storage hydro electric scheme, and the water stop. It was time to replace an hour and twenty five minutes worth of sweat.

From here things took a different turn for me with the simple process of placing one foot in front of the other becoming a dizzying effort. People I'd passed twenty minutes back were overtaking me – including the Good Samaritan. I said my tank was empty and he offered me his orange drink and a pack of jelly babies. 'Take as many as you like.' I took three, and was spurred on by the kindness and the comfort of soft chewy sweets. Ten minutes later the sugar-effect reached my legs enough to catapult me headlong down the mountain for the final stretch home. Two hours 7 minutes after starting, I crossed the finishing line, 45 minutes behind the leader – but for me, to finish was to win. S4C were covering the event and mightily relieved that a Welsh speaker from Eryri Harriers had won, as opposed to a competitor from the Shrewsbury Shufflers Running Club – an interview with subtitles is not quite the same.

I'll never forget the friendly atmosphere, the camaraderie of officials and competitors, the humility of the triumphant and the breathtaking (in more than one way) scenery. I never did get to do a London Marathon but I'm sure it would not be a patch on this.

After a couple of weeks I forgot the pain and was inspired to have a go at Ras y Gader. It translates to The Chair Race, but I can think of nothing sedentary about this, definitely not for couch potatoes. It's one of the key meets in the Welsh mountain-racing calendar from the town square in Dolgellau, up and down Cadair Idris ('Idris' chair') and the same distance and altitude gain as Ras y Moelwyn.

The legend about staying up Cadair Idris and being mad, dead or a poet by the morning, is thought to be part of a ritual or initiation as children pass into adulthood with a mix of physical and mental challenges to be overcome. I wonder if they had to run up it as well.

Ras y Moelwyn starting line
Photo: Haydn Jenkins

The atmosphere in the town square was fantastic, with Batala Bermo, the samba reggae group from Barmouth striking up a real carnival mood. Passers-by were drawn to the music with lots of swaying and foot tapping as the pulsating rhythms synchronised the anxious heartbeats of competitors bunched up at the starting line.

Up the Cadair road, through a forest alongside a lake, past the water stop at Tŷ Nant, and onto the open ground where things got steep and views stretched to distant peaks. Our final ascent was to be by the Pony Path and the ridge to Penygadair, one of the main routes to the summit and amongst the most popular with walkers. Instead of a circular route this race was an up and down and for people like myself, towards the back of the field, an opportunity to be impressed with the speed, stamina and agility of the front runners as they hurtle past you on the homeward journey.

Good paths look ancient and blend in with the landscape but they need maintaining in the face of increasing numbers of walkers, which in Snowdonia have risen by 18 per cent in the past five years. The numbers are heavily concentrated on the popular peaks such as Cadair Idris and Yr Wyddfa, whilst many of the other mountains are deserted. A lot of work had been done along our route including 'stone pitching', a traditional technique, a bit like building an underground dry stone wall to walk on top of. As I struggled up the mountain I resisted the temptation to cut corners: each footstep takes its toll on the vegetation that binds the ground together.

The rules included a cut-off point at the 2000 foot contour – failure to reach this within 75 minutes and you'd be turned back. The humiliation! I focused on achieving this milestone and made it with some minutes to spare. Fuelled up with jelly babies and encouragement from marshalls and walkers I finally made it to the top, touched the trig point and pointed downhill.

Now was not the time to take in the views, now was the time for absolute concentration on where to land the next few paces – plenty of craggy rock and loose stones to snag you but much more energy-efficient to go fast and not waste power applying the brakes. As we got below the tree line the gradient eased up and my legs took this as a cue for cramp. The flat stage through the forest was hard going, churned up by the passage of so many runners the mud was clawing at my feet. Back on to the Cadair road and a decent incline to beckon me to the finish.

After 2 hours and 21 minutes I was back where I started, with a great feeling of achievement that I had survived the challenge, neither dead nor a poet but maybe slightly mad. I might not have been able to appreciate the finer points of botany or geology but I can look back on my mountain racing days and say 'I was there'.

Water

To say it's important is an understatement. This is the habitat we evolved from and typically represents 55% to 60% of the human body. In a crisis we can survive several weeks without food but only three days without water. It's easy to take it for granted with two thirds of the earth's surface covered by water.

In the past there was a balance between man and water. There was only so much we could do to pollute it, and nature was able to put things right. But since industrialisation, the exploding world population and chemical-based agricultural methods the balance has become precarious.

Maintaining that balance is difficult. Whilst the following stories illustrate an improving trend in the waters of Wales, sadly this is not the case across the world, to the detriment of many species and ultimately to the people polluting one of life's essentials.

Pearl mussels and the generation gap

There used to be hundreds of thousands of freshwater pearl mussels in Afon Conwy, but now there are just eighty, and half of them have gone for a long stay at the Mawddach hatchery near Dolgellau, where they are part of an emergency breeding programme to save them from extinction.

These mussels are huge, up to 15 cm long, which is not surprising as they are between eighty and a hundred years old. They are the ultimate ageing population with a complete lack of succession. The males might fertilise the eggs and maybe juveniles are born but that's where it stops. Baby mussels have not survived, leaving an eighty-year generation gap in the Conwy river.

The catastrophic decline of pearl mussels is not confined to northern Wales, where numbers have dropped by 40 per cent in just the last ten years. In the same period the much smaller population in rivers of southern Wales has dropped by up to 90 per cent. The only healthy populations to be found in Britain are in the Scottish Highlands.

These mussels have been raided for their pearls since Roman times, but with the odds against finding a pearl of 500-1, that's an awful lot of crushed shells to make a necklace. This must have been a boom and bust industry as river populations got decimated, taking many years for stocks to recover. Such exploitation – now illegal, of course – does not account for the current demise of the young.

The mussel lifecycle is complex. Adults release larvae, called 'glochidia', into the river in summer and these attach themselves to the gills of young salmon and trout. The following spring, as the water warms up, they drop off the fish and settle on the riverbed to grow.

Could one reason for the decline be a lack of young fish to live on? Certainly the hatcheries have to work hard to boost the populations in our rivers. Fish no longer reproduce at anywhere near the rate they used to. Maybe this is another symptom of the same problem.

The finger of blame points mainly towards the careless use of fertilisers to sustain intensive farming. WMD – Weapons of Mussel Destruction. Unless carefully applied, the fertiliser can run off or leach into the rivers, causing a surge in the growth of aquatic plant life, tainting the clear water, and starving shellfish of oxygen. Synthetic chemicals such as sheep dips and other veterinary products may be having a detrimental effect. Phosphates from household detergents will also contribute to the problem.

Ill-considered best intentions can sometimes have disastrous consequences.

Baby pearl mussels through the microscope
Photo: Keith Scrivens

The excavator on the Afon Ddu did a great job of tidying up the river – but unwittingly scooped out 5,000 pearl mussels.

Pearl mussels don't travel far, and the young spend their first few years buried and feeding in the gravel beds. The grown-ups tend to stay put – they have a well-developed foot that they use to move around and anchor themselves to the river bed, and in times of flood they will find a secure haven to save themselves from being dashed against rocks or washed downstream.

Generally speaking a mussel in one river will remain there, which means each river will have its own unique genetics particularly suited to the conditions. For this reason mussels will only be returned to where they came from, and at the hatchery there is careful segregation of the different gene pools.

Each batch of breeding mussels lives in a small tank, with a constant flow of clean fresh water passing through into a much larger tank of fish fry. The water washes the fertilised larvae into the fish tank, where they attach themselves to the gills of the young fish. The following spring the larvae, having morphed into microscopic mussels, drop off and are transferred to rearing trays.

The juveniles are very small and will not be ready for release until they are about eight years old. At present the mortality rate in the crèche is exceedingly high, with only 1 in 700 surviving to the age of three, but maybe that's to be expected for such pioneering work, and more batches are being reared to create a viable rescue plan for these endangered molluscs.

Is this a conservation priority? To see any species disappear is a disaster and will have a knock-on impact. If millions of mussels filter water non-stop for a hundred years, surely this will create much purer water – which in turn will encourage salmon to return, and which will encourage anglers and tourists back to our rivers.

As someone whose water supply comes off the mountain I am forever needing to change or clean the filters. I wonder if I could establish a colony of pearl mussels upstream from my house and harness a natural, self-sustaining filtration system?

Welsh otters

Driving home on a rainy winter's night I saw an otter playing in a flooded ditch by the lane that runs along the river. It carried on for about a minute unperturbed by the headlights or the noise of the engine. It was me who was most affected by the chance meeting – I'd never seen an otter before.

A friend said I should report my sighting and I did. This obviously showed a wildlife interest to be encouraged, and I received an invite to a workshop organised by the Snowdonia Mammal Group, where I learnt a great deal more about this intriguing creature and how to find one.

There's a lot of wildlife out here in Snowdonia, but most of us see just the tip of the iceberg. We have a pretty good idea of the birds because they show off in front of us during the day, but mammal life is mainly nocturnal, going about its business when we're fast asleep. We can only guess or imagine what's out there, unless we know what we're looking for.

Britain's otter population began to plummet in the 1950s. Hunters were blamed, but the single biggest cause of their demise was the pollution of our rivers and streams through chemicals. In Wales this might have been due to sheep dip, and in other parts of the country through herbicides and pesticides. Being at the top of the food chain, otters were particularly vulnerable to the build-up of toxins.

Hunting was outlawed in 1981, and in recent times the use of chemicals has been much more tightly controlled. Slowly the waters cleared and eventually the otters staged a comeback. Nowadays otters are present on over 90 per cent of Welsh rivers, but there's still a long way to go, and it'll take a hundred years for the population to recover to its pre-1950 level.

It's not just clean water that otters need. They need food with lots of protein to fuel their hyperactive bodies and to endure the cold water. An otter will eat 15 per cent of its body weight each day, capitalising on whatever is in abundance. Spawning fish in the winter are relatively easy prey in small upstream pools, while frogs and frogspawn in ditches, bogs and ponds make a feast in early spring, perfect timing for the arrival of cubs. Sea sticklebacks are plentiful in the autumn.

Otters are opportunistic hunters and the ducks on Llyn Mair above Plas Tan y Bwlch have not been spared. At night time the ducks seek sanctuary in the middle of the lake by floating beyond the reaches of hungry foxes, but they are still vulnerable to the night time stealth of otters. For hunting in the dark the otters are equipped with large whiskers that detect vibrations in the water. Having said that, is it just a coincidence that the white ducks have gone first? A similar pattern

Building a two-room otter holt at Coed y Brenin

emerged with the koi carp at Portmeirion: these days you will only see the darker-coloured specimens.

Otters have also been munching on lesser horseshoe bats that have been hanging too close to the ground during hibernation. This is a bit of a conservation dilemma.

The dog otter generally has two or three females that he breeds with and will jealously guard his patch against all comers. Vacant territories are in strong demand, and if the dog otter falls victim to a road accident, his place will be taken by another dog whose first response will be to kill any cubs, just like a lion.

A typical territory might be a stretch of river as long as 20 miles, but the size is based upon the terrain and availability of food. In Snowdonia a territory usually includes a large number of ditches and streams, with otters travelling great distances to where the pickings are best. Remnants of marine prey have been found several miles inland on the Afon Prysor above Trawsfynydd – this otter must have been moving fast or suffering from constipation.

The best way of knowing whether otters are around is to find a pile of spraint, which is the name for otter poo – black tarry stuff with a very distinctive smell that has been variously described as jasmine tea or even Bombay duck. Usually it contains lots of amphibian or fish bones and scales.

The spraints are deposited at prominent sites, on large boulders or the base of tree trunks and in places that mark the boundaries of an otter territory. Beneath a bridge is a popular site, as the spraint is less likely to be washed away by the rain. If there's nothing obvious to do it on, the ever resourceful otter will build a small sandcastle and do it on that.

People often confuse our native otter with the mink, but the differences are great. The mink, which was introduced from America, is much smaller than the otter, blacker, and with minimal whiskers. Its tracks are about half the size of an otter and instead of spraints it deposits scats (another word for poo). The scats are black and shiny, full of fur, long and twisted, and stink. It's nowhere near as good a swimmer and less than 10 per cent of its diet is fish.

Another thing the otters need is a decent place to live, especially if they are going to mate and rear a family. An otter home is called a holt, and the ideal spot is under the roots of old riverbank trees. But alas, man has tidied away many of these to improve the flow of rivers and reduce the risk of floods.

To give the first-time home-buyers a leg up I took part in an otter holt-building event in Coed y Brenin. We opted for a two-room, two-door log cabin design to allow the mother peace and quiet from the cubs. The delightful riverside residence was camouflaged under a pile of twigs lashed down to stop them being washed away in floods.

Building a holt is helpful but long-term survival and regeneration of this species is closely linked with the way we look after the water and the consequent availability of otter food.

The national park's training centre at Plas Tan y Bwlch holds conservation courses at what was the stately home to the Oakeley family. As I sat in the plush surroundings of the old drawing room my eyes drifted from the slideshow to the oak relief sculpture above the massive fireplace and there, stuck on a long spear, was an otter with the huntsman surrounded by his pack of baying dogs. It is a beautiful carving of a gruesome scene in an ironic setting.

Gwyniad

An Ice Age is a tricky time for wildlife: if you don't move quick enough you can get cut off and trapped from the rest of the world. This is what happened to the gwyniad, a fish unique to Llyn Tegid or Lake Bala. But at least it was trapped in a safe haven, and so far it has flourished.

The gwyniad is a herring-like fish, typically half a pound in weight. It's a genetically different variation of the species which in Scotland is called the powan and in England the Schelly. It needs deep cold water, and Llyn Tegid, being 120 feet deep, is Wales' largest natural lake and an ideal location. The River Dee flows out from the lake but this is not a viable route for gwyniad to make contact with their close relatives in Loch Lomond!

Each February the fish come to the surface by the shores to spawn, but apart from then they stay deep down feeding on plankton. Needless to say they are a protected species but occasionally anglers will hook one and reel it to the surface. Whilst everyone does their best to return them quickly to the water, the shock and the sudden change in pressure can kill them.

Counting gwyniad is not easy, but the population is estimated to be several thousand.

So far so good, but having all your eggs in one basket, or fish in one lake, is a risky situation. One big pollution incident, maybe an airplane crash, could wipe out the entire population. The odds on that happening are pretty remote, but other threats are very real and present.

The gwyniad doesn't have the lake to itself. Whilst it co-exists happily with salmon, trout, grayling and pike, in recent years it has come under threat from a fish called the ruffe, which feeds on the eggs. It is thought that the ruffe was brought here by fishermen using it as live bait.

The biggest threat and worry comes from the rising levels of algae brought about through the run-off of nutrients, typically from fertilisers and sewage, within the catchment area. The consequent algae reduces the amount of oxygen, encroaches on the spawning grounds, and favours other types of fish.

To reduce the threat to this unique species a number of actions have been put in place to improve the quality of the water. Additionally a satellite colony is being established at Llyn Arenig, a nearby lake, to spread the risk.

It's not a simple matter of netting a couple of hundred fish and moving them 5 miles up the road - migration is by translocation of fertilised eggs.

During February in recent years, when the fish rise up from the depths for

Two gwyniad and one ruffe
Photo: Arwel Morris

spawning, about a hundred are caught in nets. Curiously the lake warden says they smell of cucumbers.

Experts strip the eggs from the females and milk the sperm from the males. The eggs are fertilised and transported in flasks to Llyn Arenig Fawr, where they are placed in an incubation tank with something that looks like astroturf at the bottom, which is a good surface for them to stick to. The tank is enclosed in perspex to exclude hungry salmon and trout, but with a couple of small holes that act as an escape hatch as and when the fish are ready to swim out. The tank is then secured 3 feet beneath the water.

How are things going at the satellite colony? It's probably a bit like sending humans to a far flung galaxy, and we won't know for a while, but fingers crossed these migrants or refugees will succeed. Up until a while ago I had no idea of the existence of this fish but if we were to lose it I would be very sad - yet another nail in the coffin or indicator that we are messing up big time.

The nuclear hare and the hydro tortoise

Sustainable energy production is vital to the well-being of the planet, and in Snowdonia there is a long history of harnessing the power of water to drive industrial machinery such as woollen mills, slate mills and pumps for the mining industry. The industries and their machines may have gone but water power still plays its part.

The hydropower station at Maentwrog has been generating electricity since 1928, and is planned to continue operating until 2088. It's only half-way through its working life. This compares with the twenty-six years of the nuclear power station at Trawsfynydd, which stopped generating in 1991 and will not be totally decommissioned until 2098!

The Maentwrog station was built in 1928 by the North Wales Power and Traction Company, which also built hydro stations at Dolgarrog and at Cwm Dyli, between Beddgelert and Capel Curig. The 'Traction' part of the company name reflected their then controlling interests in the Ffestiniog, Welsh Highland, and Snowdon railways, and the idea was to supply them with electricity.

When it opened it had sufficient capacity to satisfy the electricity requirements for all of northern Wales. Today we use a great deal more electricity, and the station supplies just the areas in and around Porthmadog, Blaenau Ffestiniog, Dolgellau and Harlech.

As I walked from the car park to the entrance someone had pressed the button, releasing the water with a huge gurgle and whoosh as it rushed down the hill into the turbines. From that point the electricity for our homes was coming from the power of local water as opposed to via the anonymous national grid.

The water for Maentwrog comes from the Trawsfynydd reservoir, which, measured in surface area, is the largest in Wales. Seventy per cent of the water is from the Afon Prysor and the rest from a series of leats that extend the catchment area to 35 square miles.

Depending on how wet the ground is, 1 inch of rain equates to between 12 and 18 inches on the dam wall. Each inch in the reservoir converts to 2 hours of generation, and in a year of average rainfall there's enough to generate 8 hours every day.

Hydro is capital-expensive but very low-cost to run with minimal manpower. These days the workforce is down to just seven people working a Monday to Friday day shift. If there's a need to start or stop generating in the middle of the weekend, this can be done remotely by the station manager's laptop over a mobile phone.

A lot of effort is required to look after the catchment, checking and unblocking the supply leats, clearing drainage ditches, monitoring dam walls and, of course, the pipe. This delivers water to the turbines at nearly 4,600 gallons per second. Falling 600 feet over 2 miles it creates a good head of pressure!

In terms of safety there's not a lot to go wrong in a hydro scheme. The worst thing that can happen is the dam wall breaking, which is what happened to the Eigiau dam in 1925. Building regulations and technology

Through turbines and onwards to the sea

have improved a lot since then, and the main dam wall at Trawsfynydd was re-built in 1988 to replace the previous dam which was suffering from a 'concrete cancer'.

1988 was also the year in which the most serious incident happened at Maentwrog. A leak in the pipe caused a substantial mudslide which engulfed a house just behind the power station. Fortunately no-one was hurt but the scar on the hillside is still there to be seen.

The annual internal check of the pipeline is probably the most important operation of the year and takes several weeks. In preparation, the reservoir is drained to its lowest level ready to catch and hold any unseasonal rainfall during June and July.

Whilst the station manager is targeted to generate as much electricity as possible, and a full reservoir makes the process more efficient, he takes great care to look after the little ringed plovers. In recent years these small birds have started using the shallow end of the lake to build their nests close to the shoreline. The last thing they want in April and May is a sudden rise in water level as they incubate their eggs, so during these months the level is kept reasonably low.

So does 160 years of hydro power generate more than twenty-six years of nuclear? Despite its longevity Maentwrog will only have generated 3 per cent of that created by Trawsfynydd but it won't take a hundred years and £1 billion to decommission!

Plant Life

Bracken, gorse and heather are plain to see but if you look more closely there is a rich mix of plant life in Snowdonia. Some are just clinging on whilst others are thriving as growing conditions adjust in their favour.

The reason for the rich mix is the diversity of habitats brought about by the mountains, their range of altitudes and consequent temperatures, and the varied composition of underlying rocks, each yielding its own growing environment. Steep-sided mountains and rock ledges also provide safe havens from hungry sheep, which significantly impact on plant life.

It is no surprise that the conservationist's map of Snowdonia is splattered with Sites of Special Scientific Interest (SSSIs) and National Nature Reserves (NNRs), homes to many rare species.

Arctic alpines in Snowdonia

Snowdonia is home to many species of arctic alpine plants. As the name suggests, these plants are best suited to the Arctic, but also thrive in mountain ranges such as the Alps where they are prolific. A friend recently took a holiday in Slovenia and described watching a farmer mowing his alpine meadow: 'With one swish of the scythe he cut more alpines than in the whole of Snowdonia!'

Whilst that's a sweeping exaggeration, the importance of the Snowdonia colony is that it's an outpost at the limits of European distribution and what happens here, and in the Brecon Beacons, is an early warning system of climate change. Changes witnessed here will move into the higher altitudes of the Alps and further north towards the Arctic with each degree of global warming.

In general these plants require a cool and shaded spot well away from the jaws of hungry sheep and goats. The north-facing cliffs of tall mountains provide this. They also provide a habitat in which the alpines are free from competition from more aggressive plants that would swamp them.

The Snowdon Lily
Photo: Peter Llewellyn

Most species also require 'base rich' material, which any gardener in Snowdonia will tell you is hard to come by. But there are pockets here and there where volcanoes 200 million years ago have thrown pyroclastic rock to the surface. This rock is rich in calcium and easy to crumble, a bit like pumice stone. It breaks off in your hand and can be ground to a powder between finger and thumb. As the rain and winds relentlessly beat upon it, a steady trickle of nutrients is released for hungry plants.

At the end of the last Ice Age arctic alpines would have progressively colonised northwards as the ice retreated remaining only in those places where the right conditions remained, creating pockets of isolated communities.

The Snowdon Lily is our best-known plant, discovered in the seventeenth century by Edward Lhuyd, hence the Latin name *Lloydia Serotina*. Its nearest neighbours are hundreds of miles away in the Alps, but surprisingly it is absent from Scotland. There are two theories as to why. Either the cold weather retreated too quickly, making it too warm north of Snowdonia for the plant to colonise further, or the Snowdon Lily survived the last Ice Age in a pocket free from ice, whereas in Scotland there were no such refuges.

One of the other rare plants in Snowdonia is the Tufted Saxifrage, which was down to just four specimens in the 1970s. A project to save it from extinction included taking seeds and cultivating hundreds of new plants. But this exercise has only been partially successful.

Norway has built a massive seed bank nick-named the 'Doomsday Vault', with bomb-proof doors and reinforced concrete walls a metre thick, in a hollowed-out cave on Spitsbergen. The objective is to protect against the irretrievable extinction of plants through nuclear or biological war, a meteor strike or global warming. The location has been chosen because it is far from earthquake activity and deep in the permafrost … Hopefully this won't melt!

Britain has its own Millennium Seed Bank, managed by the Kew Botanic Gardens and housed in Sussex. So far more than a billion seeds have been collected – including the Snowdon Lily and Tufted Saxifrage seeds, collected in Wales.

The conclusion is likely to be that Snowdonia no longer has the right conditions for arctic alpines with rising temperatures and winter snow a rare treat. Applying the brakes to climate change needs to be done, but will not take effect quickly enough. Sadly, I suspect many of the species will disappear along with the particular genetics evolved in Snowdonia. The best we can do is to remember they were here and preserve their seeds for a reintroduction if future conditions allow. In the meantime if you are walking the mountains please be careful what you tread on – the survival of a species may be at stake.

The lower plants

Not a very exciting name for some little-known but pretty amazing plants including lichens and bryophytes. Not a very appropriate-sounding name for things which can grow high up mountains and trees.

They are called 'lower' because they are more primitive and are survivors from the very earliest of plants to evolve over 350 million years ago.

They thrive in Snowdonia, which has an ideal habitat and climate – anything in which we excel needs further investigation, so I booked myself onto another course to find out more.

Lichens

We met the lichen expert in a forestry car park. In a good location there are masses to be seen, with typically twenty to thirty species per tree. Lichenology is not an energetic pastime – meetings of the Welsh Lichenology Society seldom move more than a hundred yards from the car park!

Lichen was all around us – on the signs, in the grass verges, on the rocks and of course in the trees. They are sandwiches of algae covered and protected in fungi, in return for which the algae does the photosynthesis and generates the nutrients for both to survive.

Rocks look and sound like an unlikely growing medium but lichens are tenacious plants: one species is capable of sending its roots half an inch into the rock. Maybe this plant would be hardy enough to survive on Mars.

Lichenologists usually carry a portable chemistry set – a couple of drops of bleach were placed on a white lichen and in an instant it changed to a bright red, thereby revealing its identity.

Trees, especially old trees in ancient woodlands, provide wonderful habitat, although close to car parks there is a very distinctive 'canine zone'. The lichen pattern changes considerably as it enters the ammonia-sprayed area beneath the level of a cocked leg.

Some lichens can tolerate high levels of pollution whilst others need pristine air, and plants are graded from one to ten, with ten requiring the purest. There are many European rare species in northern Wales – with the prevailing wind coming from across the Atlantic very little pollution gets blown in.

Our expert took us to a fine looking tree and pointed to a specimen that seemingly had heads of broccoli sprouting out of a leafy lichen. This was the exceedingly rare *Lobaria Amplyssima*, which in England is confined to just twelve trees in the Lake District and New Forest.

Lichens do not seem to harm the trees, although the best colonies tend to be on the older, declining specimens – most probably because these are losing their branch and leaf cover, making photosynthesis easier through increased sunlight. For similar reasons, conservationists have been trying to limit the amount of bracken, bramble and ivy growth in woodlands.

Bryophytes

After thirty minutes, lots of lifecycle diagrams and complex terms, I was beginning to regret asking what a bryophyte was. Seemingly it's all down to the sex lives of mosses and liverworts. A key requirement of the sex is a thin layer of water for the sperm to swim across to the female organs of the plant, which probably explains why Snowdonia is such a good place for them to procreate.

As for the difference between a moss and a liverwort – this was another question I wish I hadn't asked. Part of the explanation included whether there are leaves and, if so, how they are arranged. Both have 'spore capsules' that rise like periscopes high above the plant, awaiting the necessary nudge to release their fruits.

Armed with the basic theory, a magnifying lens and waterproofs, we stepped out into torrential rain in the woodlands above Ganllwyd. Our guide carefully plucked some strands from a common species and asked us to describe what we saw. Are there leaves? Yes. Are they arranged in rows? No, it must be a moss. Are there branches off the stem? Yes, we'd narrowed the classification down to just a few. Our guide explained the rest, with the aid of some diagrams on her waterproof notebook, and the particular requirements of this plant which needs relatively base-rich ground.

Just a few yards further on and a very different looking sample was studied. A moss called *Polytrichum* which requires acidic conditions. Yet a few more paces on and we found another variety of *Polytrichum*, which is the largest of our mosses and requires soggy conditions.

Surrounding this species was a bed of sphagnum, one of just thirty-four different types of sphagnum. The dead cells of this plant leave empty pockets that absorb water up to twenty times the weight or volume of the plant. Sphagnum was used as a wound dressing during the Crimean and First World Wars – not only was it good to soak up blood but also, due to the acidity, for its antiseptic properties. It used to be harvested off the hills of Snowdonia and exported by train to orchid growers in the south of England, until they decided that synthetic materials were less trouble.

We made our way to the waterfall where the spray created an even more humid environment. This patch was home to *Sematophyllum Demissum*, a species unique in Britain to just a few sites in northern Wales. I almost expected such a rare plant

Amazing lichens

to be fenced off, but there it was on a boulder in the middle of the footpath waiting for people to step on it.

When it comes to bryophytes, Britain, and Wales in particular, are tops, with more than a thousand different species, or two thirds of the range of plants that are found across Europe. It's not just a case of surviving but thriving and if this was an Olympic discipline, we'd be gold. As I toil away in my vegetable garden I have a new respect for the lower plants and, whilst they need hoeing out of the way to give my crops a chance to grow, I can't bring myself to call them weeds.

Diversification at Crûg Farm

Bleddyn and Sue Wynne-Jones diversified out of beef farming into plants, but what they stock is unlikely to be found elsewhere. There's no question of going to a Dobies seed catalogue: instead each autumn they head off on seed-collecting expeditions to far flung areas in countries such as Vietnam, Guatemala and Columbia.

Bleddyn explained the start: 'I was always keen to grow a few vegetables but back in 1991, in the build-up to BSE, it was time for a change. We erected the first two polytunnels and have been expanding the production area ever since. The shed that used to hold a hundred calves is now the over-wintering store, keeping the frost at bay but more importantly preventing death from the most common cause, becoming waterlogged.'

Stepping into the walled garden beside the farmhouse is like entering a botanical garden. Sarcococca from the Himalayas, climbing hydrangea from Mexico, viburnum from Japan and bamboo from China. Bleddyn pointed out the massive umbrella plants towering above: 'They are really popular, very dramatic and exotic-looking with leaves up to a metre across. Despite the tropical look they are suitably hardy for our climate.'

Over fifty expeditions on and they have brought back more than 15,000 different specimens, of which 2,500 are stocked as items for sale to customers at their farm just outside of Caernarfon. As a collection you'd struggle to keep up with the Wynne-Jones's.

Plants grown from seeds bought out of a catalogue come from a narrow range of varieties, with highly predictable results, but seeds gathered in the wild introduce tremendous diversity. 'Before bringing the seeds home, we have to strip off any debris, such as pods or the flesh of berries, and dry them. Once back at the farm, we sow them into margarine tubs, the perfect re-use of a waste product, and wait patiently. Things sometimes take quite a while. One batch of seeds took eight years to germinate and a further five to mature – this can be quite a long-haul business in more ways than the travel,' said Bleddyn.

Sue explained how seeds come in all shapes and sizes: 'On the last expedition £400 excess baggage had to be paid, mainly due to the hundred giant conkers each the size of a tennis ball. Bleddyn insisted on bringing a few contingencies just in case.' They are all neatly planted in the woodland area of the farm and in years to come could dramatically change the dynamics of a game of conkers (*Aesculus wangii*).

A bit like their Victorian predecessors, Sue and Bleddyn approach their work

Geranium Sue Crûg
Photo: Sue and Bleddyn Wynn-Jones

with an almost missionary zeal, but against the background of a world in which habitats are being compromised and destroyed on a grand scale. Several new species were recently collected from an area in northern Vietnam that was being cleared for development.

'In general we collect from mountainous areas, especially equatorial. If seeds are collected from a colder climate, such as Korea, the plants are likely to break dormancy too early and become victims of frost. Conversely plants from warmer countries keep their heads down until they are confident of fair weather and have a higher success rate. Sometimes we bring back plants which need warmth, and the nearby Treborth Botanic Gardens, with its large glasshouses, is pleased to take them on.'

As the planet warms, species from even warmer areas will become suitable for

Wales whilst others will move northwards in search of cooler conditions. Plants are great indicators of change and global warming, taking a composite view of factors such as temperature, humidity, wind and sunlight.

The bulk of the plants are grown from seeds but young plants or cuttings are also brought back. This requires a special licence and strict adherence to quarantine rules. Bleddyn explained the procedure: 'Imported plants can't be unpacked until the man from DEFRA arrives to inspect for pests and diseases. When the boxes are finally opened, it's in a locked building with an inner compartment enclosed by a fine mesh which no known insect can penetrate. All the water that drips off the plants is gathered into gutters and recycled. Any water that does need to be extracted has to be mixed with a bit of bleach and boiled before disposing. As for leaves that fall off, they are frozen for 48 hours before being incinerated.'

Looking in from outside, the quarantine room is illuminated by lamps, giving off an eerie, ultra violet glow reminiscent of a science fiction movie. But as yet there have been no triffids, as in the John Wyndham sci-fi story, and to our knowledge no ponticums, the invasive species of rhododendron that kills everything in its path.

All sorts of people come to visit and buy at Crûg Farm, including enthusiastic collectors from as far away as Japan. As an organisation the National Trust is a big customer as it seeks to restock or replenish historic gardens created in Victorian times.

'Caernarfon is a long way from customers in big cities so we have just introduced a mail order service,' Sue explained. 'The boxes have been designed with a pitched roof to avoid plants being squashed, the logic being that they are unsuitable to stack other boxes on top of! Overnight delivery costs £25 so it makes sense to fill the box with as many as possible. For those wanting instant gratification boxes can be joined together to ship specimens up to 3 metres tall.'

Some people are remembered by a plaque on a bench, some have grandchildren or streets named after them, but Sue has her own plant – the Geranium Sue Crûg. How romantic of Bleddyn. As for their Jack Russell, his memento is the Bertie Crûg Geranium – so named because of his low creeping nature. But I will remember these people for their courage to step out of the normal, to pursue a passion and survive the downturn in farming in such an inspiring way.

Wildlife

Wildlife is like a barometer for our impact on the environment. Some species have disappeared because we hunted them to extinction, such as the beaver which was too tasty and the wolf too much of a threat. Other species have vanished or suffered massive declines and it is frightening that sometimes we don't know why. Evolutionary change is one thing, but the loss of species as collateral damage whilst we 'improve' and develop the world is worrying.

Snowdonia has an important role to play as a 'wild place' where creatures and their habitats are less vulnerable to the modern world. There is some amazing wildlife to be seen but in some ways the most impressive thing is the growing number of people giving their time to understand what's happening and to restore vital habitats.

Dragons, damsels and silver-studded blues

Those long bi-plane insects, dragonflies and damselflies, come in all sorts of colours and sizes but both are part of the Odonata order. Odonata comes from the Greek meaning 'toothed jaw'. The body is made up of a head, with bulbous eyes providing 360º vision, a thorax to which the wings and legs are connected, and an abdomen with ten segments.

Damselflies are generally thin, small and more delicate-looking. When they're not flying their wings are tucked in parallel with their bodies. The two sets of wings are identical and you quite often see lots of damsels together.

By contrast the dragonflies are bigger, with a wingspan of up to 4 inches, more solitary and territorial. And when not flying their wings, which are not identical, stick out from their body. They are fantastic fliers with some reaching speeds of 38 mph and covering 85 miles in a day.

The lifecycle begins with intriguing sex. Males hang around the ponds and rivers waiting to pounce on furtive females. They have hooks at the tip of the abdomen with which they grab the females by the scruff of the neck or head, and you can often see them flying off in this tandem position. After a while the female agrees to mate and the pair adopt the 'wheel position' – having secondary genitalia at the top of the abdomen makes this practical. Some species remain coupled for several hours.

Eggs are placed on or in the water or in nearby vegetation and these hatch into nymphs. This underwater stage can last from about 12 months up to five years for some larger species in cold climates. They then clamber up nearby plants and emerge from their 'wetsuits' into the beautiful creatures we know. Life is short, just a couple of weeks for damsels and a couple of months for dragons if they're lucky. They're all definitely fair-weather fliers which only come out when it's warm, still and dry, so the season is confined to summer months.

Dragon- and damselflies have been around for ages, pre-dating the Pterodactyl by a hundred million years. They may have outlived the dinosaurs, but over the past forty years three species of dragonfly have become extinct in Britain. Tighter controls on pollution are now in place plus a much greater understanding and study of dragonfly needs. But are we doing enough?

I took part in a weekend workshop, organised by the Snowdonia National Park, to create greater awareness and more accurate recording of dragonflies and damselflies. In northern Wales there are thirty-three species successfully breeding, out of the forty-three total for UK.

Over the two days we studied detailed identification characteristics of each

The silver-studded blue needs ants and young heather
Photo: Jim Asher , Butterfly Conservation

The lifecycle begins with intriguing sex. Males hang around the ponds and rivers waiting to pounce on furtive females
Photo: Allan Brandon

species putting theory into practice with visits to Odonata hotspots. We visited a lake between Harlech and Porthmadog which is home to the only known colony of downy emeralds in northern Wales. On the day we saw but one: maybe the others were hiding.

We also visited Hafod Garegog National Nature Reserve between Penrhyndeudraeth and Beddgelert which is home to thirteen different species of dragon and damselfly, including the rare small red damselfly.

The boggy reserve is owned by the National Trust and the most north westerly outpost for raft spiders, Britain's largest spider with a leg span of 70 mm or the length of a finger. These are capable of walking on water and submerging for periods of time to protect themselves from predators. And it's no surprise that they are quite partial to the occasional damselfly!

Some butterflies are long distance travellers, with species such as the painted lady flying in from Europe and the monarch from across the Atlantic. Others tend to stay at home, never venturing far, and this makes them particularly vulnerable to adverse changes in habitat from which they can't migrate.

The silver-studded blue is one of the less mobile species confined to just six known sites in Wales including Hafod Garegog. What makes this place so special?

Doug Oliver, senior warden from CCW, explained the key requirements from the blue's perspective: 'They need ants, young shoots of non-bushy suppressed heather, and an unobstructed flight path.'

The females lay their eggs singly on stalks of heather – only where they detect suitable ant pheromones. The following spring the resultant larvae are either picked up by the ants or crawl into the nearest ants' nest, where they enjoy a warm and humid environment safely protected from predators – the ants collect protection money in the form of a sugary secretion. Each day the larvae crawl out to feed on the tender shoots of heather before pupating, sprouting blue wings, and flying off to mate and ultimately lay eggs.

To maintain suitable habitat cattle are released into the reserve during the summer to graze and stop the heather becoming engulfed by the grasses. During the winter the cattle are swapped for sheep to graze the heather to force new shoots of growth the following spring. In particular it's the erica heather that the blues most appreciate. All sounds nice and easy with nature and agriculture in a useful balance.

But the problem is gorse sprouting around and through the heather. Sheep are hungry and hardy, but even they don't like chewing through gorse, and this means the heather will get long, tough and straggly unless action is taken.

This is where conservation volunteers can be useful. Armed with loppers, thick gloves and basic instruction I joined a work party for a sunny autumn's day during which we lopped away, creating vast piles of gorse. The gorse will be back again in five years, but in the meantime the blues should have thrived, and the three discrete colonies on this site may have joined into one large colony and thereby be less vulnerable.

Each time I pass the reserve I think back to the prickly gorse and am reminded of the struggle for survival, and the complex web of dependencies which includes intervention by people. Far from being a wilderness, Wales is a highly manicured landscape shaped by agriculture, and our biodiversity or current mix of species is a product of that.

On the trail of the lonesome pine marten

There was a time when pine martens ruled the roost. Six thousand years ago, when Britain was covered by woodland, they were second only to the weasel as our most prolific carnivore. Today they are second only to the wild cat as our most rare and endangered.

The root cause of their demise is the lack of trees. Pine martens are perfectly suited to woodland making full advantage of the 3-D environment to live safely beyond the reach of foxes.

The last Ice Age left a barren landscape, but within a few thousand years we were covered in trees, the default habitat until man chops them down. By 500 BC Britain was only 50 per cent woodland and reached an all time low of 5 per cent after the extractions for the First World War.

By then the pine marten population was estimated at 2000 and confined mainly to refuges of the north west Highlands, the Lake District, and Snowdonia. Their natural habitat had been severely compromised, and for many years they were persecuted by gamekeepers protecting the likes of pheasant and grouse.

The Lord Lucan of Welsh mammals
Photo: Frank Greenaway of Vincent Wildlife Trust

The shortage of timber during the war frightened Britain into greater self-sufficiency with the establishment of the Forestry Commission in 1919 and the planting of upland forests. Nowadays Snowdonia is 12 per cent woodland. Surrey is the only county with more than 20 per cent. Compared to Europe, where the average is 46 per cent, we are relatively bald.

There are lots of pine martens in Scotland, where they are making a steady comeback and so too in the west of Ireland. In Wales there is a lot of talk but little by way of proof and knowing whether or not you've got pine martens is not easy.

The most categoric proof is a specimen, but the last dead body to be found in Wales was back in 1950.

A sighting is good evidence, especially if by someone who knows what they are looking for, but most people would struggle to tell the difference between a marten and a polecat. In the blink of an eye even a squirrel or a cat could be confusing: a recent visitor described his encounter with what looked like a skinny badger running up a tree and spent the rest of his holiday in a stake-out with camera at the ready!

The Vincent Wildlife Trust has done a lot of work to help understand and promote the return of the pine marten. One of their initiatives has been to create a process for collecting and classifying reported sightings. Essentially this involves a structured interview without leading questions such as: 'Did the animal in question have a chocolate coloured coat with a white patch on its chest?' On the basis of the interview the sighting is given a grading of 1 to 10, where 10 is a definite. Within Wales there have been more than 200 sightings since 1995 with a probability rating greater than five.

Scats (poo) are great evidence and can differentiate between a marten and a polecat. Pine marten scats smell sweet and musky, maybe crushed cranberry, whilst polecats' smell foul. Hence the animals have sometimes been called Sweet Mart and Foul Mart.

But scats can be confusing and change dramatically according to diet: a fox eating berries can produce a fine replica good enough to confuse a keen amateur.

In an effort to prove their presence in Snowdonia, the national park engaged the services of Pine Marten Pete, a specialist from Ireland. Hair tubes were mounted 5 feet up trees in woods where there had been good sightings. The tubes were baited with chicken, the idea being to lure hungry martens up the tube, leaving a few hairs on the sticky pads at the bottom of the tube. But after eighteen months the only hairs to be analysed under microscope turned out to belong to squirrels – grey ones, unfortunately – the only place where red squirrels survive in the national park is near Bala.

Efforts to track down the Lord Lucan of Welsh mammals have been stepped up with the use of modern technology. Conclusive evidence can also be obtained through DNA analysis of scats, and for this to work the scat must be fresh as it's the mucous coating that carries the DNA.

A team of thirty wildlife enthusiasts were briefed by Pine Marten Pete at the national park's training centre. The briefing began with a slideshow identity parade of scats with the most unlikely looking specimens turning out to be from martens. The archetypal scat is a hair pin or heart shaped twisted coil about the thickness of a finger, but depending on diet and the amount of weathering they can come in many shapes and sizes.

Armed with this knowledge the group split into several teams and spent their weekend scouring different parts of Snowdonia examining countless specimens and coaxing likely suspects into polythene bags, sealed, with a grid reference written on the label. A total of 131 samples were collected and bunged into the freezer to keep them fresh for transportation and analysis back in Ireland.

In a similar exercise near Aberystwyth thirty-six scats were collected, of which one was confirmed as being pine marten. By extrapolation, surely we would have three and a half? Alas, we had nothing more exciting than a lot of foxes and a miniature schnauzer – it's amazing how precise science can be and the things people will do in the pursuit of conservation. For the time being we will have to settle for the occasional sighting and the possibility that they still survive in Snowdonia.

Bats

They're not everyone's favourite creature but I think they are great, and as I share my house with a few hundred of them it's just as well to get along. I know they are around because I can see them flying out from their various roosts at dusk and the piles of droppings on the floor of the attic – not hard pellets like a mouse's, but cylinders of insect dust that crumble in your fingers. As part of getting to know and understand my new neighbours I thought it would be good to join my local bat group.

Counting bats in mines

Us humans get counted in a census each decade but bats are counted every year. On a cold winter's morning I went along with two members of the Gwynedd Bat Group to count the lesser horseshoe bats hibernating in disused slate mines.

These bats are pretty rare, with an estimated UK population of 14,000, of which half live in Wales. Conservationists want to know whether they are in decline or bouncing back, what has been the impact of ten mild winters and – one of the dilemmas – is it true that otters have been scoffing the low hanging bats? But these questions of interpretation and trends in data were not for us – our job was to count, and as accurately as possible.

Horseshoe bats get their name from the horseshoe shape appearance of their faces. The 'lesser' horseshoe is, as you can guess, a small version, about the size of a plum, whilst the 'greater' is the size of a fist. Their distinctive hibernation characteristic is that they hang upside down in caves or mines with their wings wrapped tightly around them – a bit like a duvet.

The first mine we went into was flooded and wellies were swapped for waders. Hard hats for caving were distributed, with torches that clip on top, but the most important gadget was the 'clicker', just like the device used on planes to count the number of passengers. The cabin crew make it look so easy as they walk through the plane clicking away, but for them the subjects are presented in uniform rows, as opposed to the random hangings of bats.

As I lowered myself into the water I felt the trickle of cold find its way through the cracked rubber and we waded deep into the adit, stumbling on submerged boulders, until we reached dry ground. Sounds that were faint at the entrance were amplified inside with distant lorries across the valley sounding as though they had lost their silencers. Water was dripping through the rock with silvery streaks of fool's gold glistening in the torchlight.

As we emerged from the water we started to find the bats, few and far between

Lesser horseshoe bats hang from ceilings to hibernate
Photo: John. J. Kaczanow

at first and then in larger groups. I'm not sure why but some bats had a nice quiet spot all to themselves, whilst others went for dormitory style hibernation in gangs of a dozen or more. The key to accurate counting is to be systematic, shine your torch slowly up and over from left to right and back again as you edge forward in a slight stoop to avoid banging your head – the Bat Group were not so worried about heads being banged as bats being squashed.

It sounds easy enough but it's surprising what tricks your eyes can play with all the shadows and sounds of other clickers. Have I counted this bat already? That one? Or that one? Believe it or not they all look the same, to me at least, especially in the dark.

Back outside and the scores were compared, added up and divided by the three of us to get an average. Sometimes there are just a few but in some mines there are more than a hundred – on this my first occasion we settled on a figure of ninety-six, with my hopeless undercount of sixty-something being discounted.

It is no coincidence that Snowdonia is considered to be the European stronghold for these bats. The vast numbers of disused mines and buildings have created the perfect habitat for them to flourish, one of the rare instances in which man's industrial exploitation has inadvertently benefited wildlife.

The 9 o'clock pips

Hibernation counts might be cold but at least they are midge-free. As the sun went down on a midsummer night's eve in Snowdonia we must have looked a strange bunch of people lurking outside Cobdens Hotel in Capel Curig. Reeking of Jungle Formula, garbed in midge-proof hats, and gazing intently skywards, we were ready for the annual count of the pips (pipistrelles) resident in the hotel roof, one of the UK's largest colonies of bats.

Midsummer is the time of year when the baby pips are born, from the mating of the previous autumn. It sounds like a long pregnancy for such small creatures, but in the late spring the mothers-to-be, taking account of the weather forecast, synchronise their biorhythms to begin gestation and give birth at the same time. What they are aiming for is a communal birth coinciding with the maximum availability of midges. An adult eats its way through 3000 a night, so it's as well to have a plentiful supply.

We stood guard, with each of us allocated a stretch of roof to watch the pips squeezing out through gaps beneath the gutters or bargeboards. Just after 9 o'clock the first pip took off into the dusk. A few more followed from different sections, and all was going well until near disaster: it started to rain. Bats have a high metabolic rate with a body temperature much higher than ours. The impact of the rain is that they cool down very quickly and must beat a hasty retreat back to the warm roost.

The rain eased off and the midges were buzzing in our ears, unseen in the dark but easily echo-located by hungry bats. Up in the roof the air traffic control got busy as the trickle of bats turned into a torrent. From one particular hole there were bats emerging every couple of seconds, they must have been British bats with a disciplined queue behind the bargeboards.

As dusk turned to nightfall, the flow of departures slowed right down and bats started returning to suckle their young. By 10.30 the count was deemed complete and the strange group retired to the hotel lobby, where numbers were added up to give the grand total of 1300, 40 per cent up on the previous year. The bats are not just surviving but thriving; as for the midges, my bites testify to their success and the failure of my defences.

Confused bat

They're supposed to hibernate with just the occasional sortie to gather food, but with warmer winters they just don't know whether they're coming or going. The numbers counted at hibernation roosts are reducing as the temperatures rise.

During warm spells there are frequent flyers leaving the roosts in the middle of winter.

I was talking to someone on the phone as I sat in a window seat. Concentrating on my conversation, I glanced down at the window catch and noticed a sizeable cobweb. When I tried to brush it away, it moved. It was a small bat.

At first I thought, how cute, and left it be to snooze until night time. But when I looked the following morning it was in exactly the same position, upside down on the window ledge with its head buried behind the latch. But instead of hanging on by both back feet only one was in contact with the wood with the other limply suspended in thin air.

Some species of bats can live for twenty years or more but this one looked half dead. Being a member of the Bat Group I knew to phone Sarah the expert for help. I explained that the bat was at death's door.

She could not visit until the afternoon so I was told what to do in the meantime: basically try and give it some water and keep the dog away!

I put some drops on an in-between-the-teeth brush and offered it to the bat which looked dazed, confused and pathetic. But eventually it lapped the water with its tiny tongue and then groomed its front wings.

By the time Sarah arrived the bat was back in hibernation on the windowsill. Looking so weak and feeble, I told her I thought it had not got long to go. She picked it up to examine. The wings were carefully unfolded and checked for rips and the bones for breaks but all looked sound. The rest of the body also seemed fine.

All this young pipistrelle needed was to be returned to a suitable hibernation place, out of the reach of our dog, away from the children and central heating. I was given my instructions.

As dusk fell I picked up the bat, wearing gloves of course, and held it with cupped hands. After about thirty minutes the bat started to vibrate as its body warmed up and it came back to life. It was very alert now with its eyes scanning the room.

I took it outside and let it climb onto my forearm. First the left wing was extended fully and retracted, then the other. A brief pause, a final backward glance, and off it fluttered into the trees.

I wonder if we'll recognise each other next time we meet?

Final Note
Bats are protected by law and should not be interfered with in any way. If in any doubt, please contact the Bat Conservation Trust at 020 7627 2629, or www.bats.org.uk

Farming

Farming feeds us, shapes the landscape and is rich in history and tradition. As for the farmers it's a livelihood and a way of life that typically means enduring long lonely hours, harsh weather and low prices at market. What they lack in bank balance wealth they make up for in a spirit of determination and passion for their piece of the countryside.

The economics have changed dramatically in the last hundred years or so, with ongoing consolidation of small farms into larger ones, and with one farmer trying to cover what used to be done by ten. Until recently the emphasis was on production but government subsidy is now geared towards stewardship of the land.

The viability of farming, and upland farming in particular, is very fragile and its future will depend not just upon the farmer producing quality products but us the consumers recognising – and whenever possible buying – that quality in the face of cheap supermarket alternatives from across the world.

Hafod y Llan and the National Trust

When I think of the National Trust I picture castles, stately homes, historic monuments and well-tended gardens, but Hafod y Llan's farmyard is best visited in a pair of wellies. It came as a surprise to me to learn that this was but one of more than 2000 farms owned by the National Trust. But then again, if your goal is to preserve the countryside, of which the vast majority is farmland, it's only logical that there should be a focus on farms.

Some of the farms were donated years ago along with a stately home or castle, the thinking being that the farming income would cover the costs of maintaining the grand old buildings. But the fortunes of farms, and particularly upland farms, have plummeted, with farmers struggling to make ends meet, selling livestock at 1990s prices but with the costs of today, not to mention the removal of livestock subsidies.

I suspect that Hafod y Llan is one of the more special farms in the Trust's portfolio. Near Beddgelert, rising from the Nantgwynant valley floor almost 3000 feet to the summit of Snowdon. Across the valley on the slopes of Cnicht is Gelli Iago, another substantial farm managed as part of the same 4,000 acre estate. Both were acquired in 1998, following a massive public appeal and a £1m pound donation from Sir Anthony Hopkins.

In terms of being important, Hafod y Llan ticked almost every box possible, including National Nature Reserve, Site of Special Scientific Interest, Grade II listed farmhouse and farm buildings, plus Scheduled Ancient Monuments within the grounds. If any farm was ripe for priority conservation status and attention, this was certainly the one.

With the National Trust as the owner, the objectives of the farm are much broader, more public-minded and longer-term than those of a privately owned or tenanted farm, where an individual is simply trying to make a living.

One of the key goals has been to improve the habitat which had suffered through sheep overgrazing, encouraged by government subsidies which, until recently, were based on the size of the flock. *Habitat* is a general term and the farm has been segmented into seventeen different sections containing types of habitat such as dry heath, acid grassland, blanket bog etc.

Believe it or not, sheep are very selective and picky grazers. They go for the sweet tender grasses, bilberry and heather, leaving behind a dense carpet of rank grasses which represent a very uninteresting and un-biodiverse environment. To reverse this situation and restore the land to how it might have looked a hundred years ago, the numbers of sheep have been halved and cattle re-introduced.

Pedigree Welsh Blacks, of course, which are mountain mowers eating just about anything in front of them. Additionally the weight and the hooves of the cattle break up the ground, giving other vegetation a chance to spring back. The consequence is that come the autumn, instead of a blanket covering of lime green the landscape is peppered with blooming heather and all the creatures that go with it.

To manage and control the grazing, farmers need solid boundaries, and much effort has gone into restoring the miles and miles of stone walls. Not only are these very functional and enduring, they are also attractive havens or corridors for a whole host of mammals such as stoats, weasels and voles.

Things were going pretty well until 2001 when the dreaded foot and mouth disease struck. With livestock markets closed, this potential catastrophe spurred the National Trust to launch into the direct marketing of their, by now, organic lamb, and this continues today with up to 250 lambs supplied each year. The lamb is delivered to customers' doorsteps in boxes lined with sheep's wool for protection and insulation – so much better than expanded polystyrene! These days you can also order organic Welsh Black Beef.

But if you prefer to meet and enjoy these beautiful creatures you are made very welcome. A key aspect of the National Trust's work is to make the countryside available for everyone. As well as maintaining existing footpaths, such as the Watkin Path on its western boundary, several new routes and walks have been created around the farm and connecting with other National Trust property in the area. In-depth study visits are also encouraged to share knowledge and experience, particularly with regard to innovative agri-environment practices.

A large part of the farm is mixed oak and ash woodland, which is a wonderfully rich habitat supporting more than a thousand forms of animal and plant life, including species which are rare on a European basis. These woods will naturally regenerate if goat and sheep populations can be managed and prevented from munching the tender young saplings. Excluding sheep is relatively easy, but the rapidly-growing population of wild mountain goats, and their ability to clamber over walls and fences, poses a threat to this regeneration.

Biodiversity on this farm means just about everything in moderation – apart from rhododendrons – public enemy number one, and a real pest throughout this valley. When I say rhododendrons I don't mean the beautiful ornamental ones gracing many gardens but the invasive, ponticum species which chokes everything else to death. Left unchecked, ponticum will take over at the expense of our native trees and plants.

I was lucky to be shown around the farm by Arwyn Owen, the Farm Manager, and when I asked him what the farm might look like in fifty years, he replied:

Welsh Blacks from the herd at Hafod y Llan

'Expansion of the woodland and trees higher up the mountain. More heather on the hills. But most importantly, people still living and working here, and visitors coming out to experience and enjoy this wonderful area.'

Each time I walk through the farm on the Watkin Path I am inspired by this landscape, so much a product of agriculture and not just wilderness.

Silence of the lambs in the mist

Mid July, and our neighbour's farm is the last to gather its sheep off the mountain. The sheep have been enjoying the mountain grass for the last couple of months, since the moment our farmer thought the weather was OK to send them up. But now it's time to come down for shearing.

We meet outside the farm at 5:00 a.m. The plan is to get up and down before it gets too hot. One by one the gang assembles. It's a mixture of young and not-so-young, family, other farmers, and me the neighbour. They've done this many times over the last three weeks, taking it in turns to help each other, but for me it's full of fresh excitement.

The gathering gang seems a bit subdued. One of the older men has stretched himself out on a sack of wool and seems to be asleep. There's a lot of muttering and cursing about the weather. It's fine where we are, but clouds are covering the top of the mountain.

Most farm jobs carry on whatever the weather, but cloud on the mountain is a no-no for gathering the sheep. Fluffy grey sheep blend in perfectly with the clouds, making them impossible to see at any distance. You can't see your colleagues as you sweep the mountain from different directions. You can't see the dogs to guide and control them. Apart from these complications there is also the safety hazard: there are many cliffs waiting to catch you out.

From where we are by the river, we are right up against the foot of the mountain and can only see the first ridge. Dafydd phones his wife, who has a good view from her kitchen: 'Yes, you can see it now. Hold on. No, it's gone again. I think it'll clear soon ...' Geraint gets into his van and listens to the weather forecast. It's too general, whilst what's happening on our mountain right now is a bit too specific. The farmer takes off in his Land Rover and watches from the other side of the valley as we kick our heels in the farmyard. There's only so much small talk welcome this early.

The dogs are getting restless and are let out to stretch their legs. What a canine social event this is. So many tyres from so many farms to be sniffed and a leg cocked against. There's a lot of competition and status amongst the assembled pack, and some need reminding who's top dog.

At 10 o'clock, the farmer comes back from yet another recce. 'Amser paned' ... let's get a cup of tea. Ten of us squeeze into the farmhouse and are made very welcome. Tea, sausage rolls, bread and cake ... great, feel fit to tackle a mountain now.

It's decided that now is the time to go. I climb into the back of a 4x4x4, where

Gathering the sheep off Moelwyn Bach for shearing in July

the last 4 indicates the number of sheepdogs I have for company. Three of us and the four dogs are taken to the west, whilst the larger group of seven with eleven dogs are dropped off to the east of the mountain.

We climb part-way up a ridge before splitting up. I'm to make my way to the point where the wall comes down from the mountain and ignore the blue-marked sheep – they've crossed over the top of the mountain from another farm. I can hear the dogs being worked above me but otherwise it's peace and quiet. Not many sheep here, just a few wild goats watching on.

I make it to the wall, driving a couple of sheep ahead. The man above is now in position with his dogs and shouts down. It's going to be a long wait, as the cloud has come down again whilst the farmer is out of sight scouring the top. Eventually the cloud lifts and we're on the move again. Sheep that were in twos or threes are now in tens or more, moving cautiously downwards and towards the centre of the mountain.

Gathering is never an exact science nor a complete sweep, there's always one or more that gets away. A shaggy one with the front of her coat hanging down stands defiant in front of two dogs. She stamps her feet and snorts at them, before dashing recklessly diagonally down the mountain in the wrong direction. The dogs follow as the sheep rebounds off a stone wall and carries on relentless. This sheep is too determined and gets left behind; so much for the parable of the lost sheep.

By now the sun has burnt through the early morning clouds and is beating down with a vengeance. The lower we get the hotter we get. Sheep, dogs and shepherds are converging downwards from all directions. Just below me a sheep is trying to hide in the undergrowth, too exhausted to go any further. One of the men carries her on his shoulders – hardly a 'piggy-back'!

As we descend we move from the cliffs, through boulder fields into the heather belt, the bogs and thence into the bracken. If the sheep kept silent and still, thousands could hide away beneath this tall green camouflage. It's an exhausting job for dogs to break through the forest of bracken.

Having undergone all kinds of natural hazards, we are just about to cross the line of the Ffestiniog Railway when an unscheduled train comes past. A couple of minutes later and there would have been either an emergency stop or a few lamb chops.

More or less back at the farm and the dogs take a muddy bath and a few mouthfuls of brackish water. Their work is almost done, whereas the shepherds have many hours of shearing ahead of them.

What sort of future lies ahead for this type of farming? With the demise of subsidies, the rising costs of labour and materials, the lack of young blood into the business and the relentless competition from overseas, its economic viability and likelihood of survival are far from certain. The going is certainly going to be tough. I'm glad I've had the privilege to take part in a gathering, but I'm not sure my grandchildren will have such an opportunity.

Alpine farming

When I think of alpine farming I conjure up a picture of Heidi, *Sound of Music,* muesli and lots of snow, but I was surprised to discover that it's a tradition that survived in Snowdonia up until about 1800.

In medieval times hill farming would have been more 'free range', with shepherds moving livestock around open mountain land. Predators, such as wolves and eagles and even poachers, would have necessitated bringing the small flocks into folds at night and constant guarding.

This roving approach formed part of the 'hafod a hendre' tradition of alpine style farming, taking advantage of fine weather and high pastures during the summer and enabling the more fertile lower ground to be cultivated. 'Hafod' translates to *'summer house'*, whilst 'hendre' translates to *'old home'* or *'winter dwelling'*.

The date for moving up the mountain was not any old summer's day but Calan Mai (May Day), and the livestock and at least part of the farmer's family would live up here, tending and milking the cows and carrying the milk or cheese down to the customers. As for the end of summer this was Calan Gaeaf or All Souls Day on the 1st November. Farming was an integral part of the Celtic calendar, and linked with pagan traditions.

Alpine farming died out when the emphasis switched away from cattle to sheep production and the hafotai (plural of hafod tŷ) became upland farms in their own right. There are many roofless derelict barns in the mountains with gaps in the stonework where beams would have supported the upper floor that housed the hay. Looking around at the endless bracken and gorse it's difficult to imagine a hay crop being harvested in this wilderness but a long time ago it was all carefully managed, people depended upon it for their sustenance and livelihood.

I was equally surprised to discover that Snowdonia has an alpine twin in Slovenia, the Triglav National Park. Both countries are small with their own unique language and have national parks named after iconic mountains with Triglav, meaning 'three heads', rising almost three times as high as Snowdon. Since 1993 these two national parks have been twinned to exchange information and learn from each other.

Slovenia is a relative newcomer to the European Union and under pressure to develop and modernise but still has remnants of alpine farming. Close to the Italian border there is a summer farm high up in the mountains. In June, after the lambs have gone to market, two hundred and sixty ewes are released up into the

Alpine sheep in Slovenia keen for milking

high altitude pastures, some more than double the height of Snowdon, with lower pastures being used in poor weather.

Each evening the sheep and a herd of goats are shepherded to the farm. You can hear the tinkle and clanking of their bells from far away but one absent sound is the barking of sheepdogs, not used for fear the dogs would scare them over a cliff. It's difficult to imagine my neighbour the farmer gathering sheep without dogs and a lot of swearing – commands in Welsh, with curses in English passed off as 'French'!

The Slovenian sheep are milked by hand by the five farmers working together as a co-operative and sharing the milking according to the number of sheep they own, a farmer with seventy sheep will put in seventy days of milking during the season. As for the goats they are milked last and kept separate from the sheep to avoid fights. After a night in the barn and early morning milking the animals are turned out into the pasture and the daily cheese production gets under way.

Goats' milk is added to the sheeps' milk to enhance the flavour, heated up in a copper cauldron over a log fire and made into great big rondels of cheese. At the start of the summer the flock yields about three hundred litres of milk per day, whilst by the end of August this is down to a hundred litres. At the end of the short season two tonnes of cheese will have been produced and sold for about £20,000.

The making of hay is small scale, and typically with a scythe or walk-behind mower. Just as Snowdonia has plenty of rain so too has Triglav where they say 'the rain has children' and this poses a problem for drying the hay. The Slovene farmers overcome this with racks a bit like a clothes rack with a gabled roof, and in this way the hay can be made whatever the weather

Hay was also made in the lower of the mountain pastures and transported down on sledges after the first snowfall – no pulling was needed, the farmers would hold onto the high handles at the front of the sledge with their backs pressed against the hay, digging their heels into the snow to apply the brakes.

One big difference between Triglav and Snowdonia is the underlying rock, which in Slovenia is predominantly soft limestone yielding nutrients more easily than our hard granite and slate. The knock-on effect is a lush pasture full of wild flowers. Another big difference in the landscape is the woodland which covers 67 per cent compared to the 12 per cent of Snowdonia, and with a tree line three times higher than ours at 1800 metres.

I was enjoying a cool drink in a village café as the afternoon drew to a close and the sound of cowbells got closer and closer. Munching as they went, the cows ripped into rich clumps of herbs, perfuming themselves with wild thyme. Someone opened the gate from the bottom pasture and the cattle moved slowly to the village centre, peeling off one by one to their respective barns, pausing to sniff at hanging baskets and chivvied along by old women wielding long sticks.

It's unlikely that this idyllic picture rooted in the past will survive the pressures and constraints of our modern world but maybe one day there will be a revival of these sorts of traditions in Snowdonia.

I think it's great that two of my favourite places should be twinned, sharing many aspects of similar heritage, and I hope the alpine farming tradition, long dead in Snowdonia, will be kept alive by those few Slovenian farmers embracing a way of life that flies in the face of a modern economy. Maybe we should invite the Slovenians for an exchange visit, and provide subsidies for milking stools and copper cauldrons, to help us reinstate our lost tradition.

It's a goat's life

Snowdonia is home to an estimated 2000 wild mountain goats, a throwback to Neolithic farmers who introduced them thousands of years ago. Ideally suited to the rugged terrain and with multiple uses – not just for their meat and skin or milk and cheese, but also tallow for candles and even judges' wigs.

About 200 years ago the farming emphasis switched to sheep and wool production, and in the changeover lots of goats were released or escaped into the wild. Nowadays they roam the mountains, many of them considered to be 'primitives' or direct descendants of the original stock as opposed to hybrid versions that have interbred with modern pedigrees.

A few years ago I embarked on a project to restore my old walled garden in the foothills of Moelwyn Bach. The wall was quite high inside the garden but low on the outside and, with just a few strands of rusty wire on top, was far from stock proof.

During the first year I cultivated a couple of sections and built up huge piles of brambles and bracken roots. A massive Scots Pine, which lay sprawled across much of the garden, needed sawing and moving to the log shed. Ancient damson trees had sent out hundreds of suckers, some of which were thirty year old trees in their own right. Much chopping and root-pulling later and the patch was beginning to look respectable.

That first season I put in a few crops to see what would grow, and some success was had with runner beans, potatoes, red cabbage and chard, whereas carrots and onions were like African drought crops.

Another reason for planting was to see whether our local goats would have a go. Goats are by nature local and are hefted (instinctively tied to an area) to just a couple of miles from where they are born, with the billies straying a bit farther in the rutting season. The number of goats in our local family has fluctuated between six and nine and I've given some of them names. One of them is called Legless. I helped rescue her when she got herself snagged on a fence and for several weeks she lost the use of both back legs. Our neighbouring farmer created a small pen for her, administered medicine and provided fresh forage with the rest of the goats visiting and calling out to her every day. After several weeks she hopped out of the pen and limped after the rest of the family. Maybe it was because of my good deed that the goats left my vegetables alone that first year?

Come the second summer I had a much bigger patch under control with terracing beneath the far walls. Ambitious planting plans included herbs galore, potatoes, various beans and peas, carrots, leeks, parsnips, lettuces, purple sprouting, courgettes, pumpkins, fruit trees and currant bushes. A garden of Eden was in the making.

Things were coming along quite well despite the slugs and by mid-June the young fruit trees were looking fit and healthy, full of blossom. The strawberries had been moved to a new bed and were settling in nicely. Red currant and white currant bushes were sprouting forth – but then disaster struck.

I arrived home one evening to find the goats munching their way through the garden. Grabbing a large stick I gave chase to them uttering various curses. They left quickly, apart from the two-month-old kid, who took some time to find her escape route – the adults went over the top but she squeezed through a gap.

Young fruit trees had been stripped and snapped off. Strawberry plants had been swallowed whole. Currant bushes had received a crew cut. The runner bean wigwam was vandalised. Fortunately they didn't fancy the potatoes, sweet peas, artichokes and purple sprouting.

Undeterred I set about building serious defensive measures to exclude the goats for my third season. The walls were topped with fencing and

Wild goats enjoying my wigwam of beans and sweet peas

extensions put on gates to make a 6-foot barrier all round. The fence posts were placed pointed side up – I didn't want the farmer thinking I'd done that by accident, so I painted the tips different colours to make them look like crayons.

With even more ground under cultivation and extensive planting the garden must look like an oasis to the wild goats, but touch wood, there have been no subsequent invasions. Maybe the crayons scared them off? Or are they waiting for some better crops?

Each winter I take part in the annual goat census which takes place over several days on different mountain ranges. Results show rapidly increasing numbers on the back of successive mild winters, with a higher incidence of surviving twins. As numbers increase so does the conflict with landowners complaining about the damage, primarily to woodland regeneration, and calling for action to reduce the population and its impact.

Contraception is used to limit the numbers of Kashmiri goats living wild on the Great Orme, but in open countryside this is impractical. Capture and transportation is another method which has been used albeit this is difficult and not without stress to the animals. Fencing is OK for my small garden but on a landscape scale would be out of the question. The only practical option, yet one that provokes highly emotional outcries of protest and threats against the organisers, is shooting by marksmen.

Goats used to be slaughtered like other farm livestock and occasionally a wild one would be shot and served up to helpers at shearing time. The culling of deer takes place every year in the forest at Coed y Brenin to maintain a sustainable population, yet this goes unnoticed and unprotested. But when it comes to goats, logic and reason seemingly go out of the window. It's as if they have taken on a mystical symbolism of wild Wales to be defended at all costs. I can see the need for controlling numbers and that the marksman is probably the best of the short straws but I don't think I could pull the trigger on my neighbours.

Local Produce

I know we are reminded that we should 'eat to live' as opposed to 'live to eat', but food is much more than just a means to survival, it's an important part of our cultural heritage and part of what makes us different.

Wales the land of music, poetry or rugby are labels that sit comfortably, but why not the land of food? When it comes to Michelin stars we trail Scotland, with just two to their twelve, yet in terms of raw ingredients we have some of the best. What's more, it's on our doorstep, with no need to travel halfway round the world.

As for the connection between local farming, food and people, this is a supply chain that needs fixing for everyone's sake. On the third Sunday of the month the farmers' market in the town square in Dolgellau is a great place to experience such a chain, to meet and talk to local producers and to taste and buy their food.

The various tastings made me hungry, and the smell of freshly roasting lamb emanating from what looked like a burger stall was more than I could endure. My bap was filled to brimming with chunky slices of meat and a topping of mint sauce served by Margaret and Maldwyn Thomas, the farmers who graze their sheep on the Aran mountains. Slowly matured local organic lamb as a 'fast food' would make for a great franchise across Wales.

Saltmarsh lamb

Welsh mountain lamb is renowned for being small but tasty, and this reflects their hardy environment. Saltmarsh lamb from the picturesque estuaries of Snowdonia is a speciality, with a taste much sought-after by the French – to whom most of our Welsh production is exported.

Rick Stein served *agneau pré-salé* (saltmarsh lamb to you and me) to Jacques Chirac at an Anglo-French summit to celebrate the President's birthday. The Frenchman's gourmet credentials were questioned as he glugged German lager with the meal, but maybe this was a diplomatic culinary snub.

You don't have to go to France or to Downing Street to appreciate it: you can buy from your local butcher or by mail order, albeit only when it's in season, which is from June until October. Of course, it wouldn't be so special if you could get it any time of the year.

I bought our family a leg of saltmarsh lamb, paying about 10 per cent more than for mountain lamb, and took it home with great anticipation. I took it out of its wrapping and studied the joint, leaner than I expected and a darker colour.

On the principle of not seasoning food before you taste it, I forewent the usual custom of squeezing slices of garlic into the flesh. This was to be *au naturel,* apart from the rosemary.

Roasted for an hour at 200°C with a couple of turns then rested under foil for fifteen minutes until ready for carving. Slices slipped off the sharp knife and served with roast potatoes, freshly picked and podded broad beans and peas, with a chilled mint sauce. *Magnifique!*

Had I been blindfold, I like to think that I would have been able to taste the difference. It was more tender than I am used to and the flavour lingered for longer. I can't describe how, but the taste was different, maybe all the pleasant bits were amplified.

On the basis that 'sheep is what sheep eats' it is not surprising that it tastes so good. The 'saltings' or 'sea meadows' alongside the estuary are abundant in saltmarsh grasses, samphire, sea lavender and thrift. It sounds such an attractive mixed salad. The location of the meadows means the land has never been 'improved' with ploughing, reseeding and fertilising, so what the sheep get is an entirely natural and diverse diet.

Contrary to my naïve expectation the meat was not salty. The grasses, such as Spartina, are tolerant to the salt conditions because they have glands with which to excrete the excess salt. From the farming point of view the tidal purge of salty water is of great benefit, killing most of the parasitic worms and bacteria that can be

Saltmarsh lambs

harmful to sheep and thereby reducing the need to treat them with expensive chemicals.

There's something inherently nice about animals being free-range, but to be free-range beside the sea sounds even better, with the bracing Atlantic air and the regular exercise routine each time the tide turns. It's as if the dominant sheep in the flock senses when the tide is coming in, and leads the flock in a long line up the estuary to the higher ground, returning as it goes out.

While I was at the butcher's waiting to be served a woman from Kent was having a cool bag filled with meat to take home. Kent might be the garden of England, but when it comes to meat there's nothing to touch Welsh produce from a traditional family butcher.

Glyn Davies has been working here for twenty-six years and took over the business from his uncle. 'People are so much more aware of their food and where it comes from. They're much more picky these days. Tescos came to the area a few years ago but far from damaging our business we have been able to grow. English customers are among the most supportive – maybe they are richer and can afford to shop where they like, but I think it's also because they've lost their local butchers and know what they're missing'.

Fork to fork just fifty yards

Years ago I lived in Croatia, just as it split apart from Yugoslavia. Our kitchen was well-equipped and with recipe books full of wonderful ideas for me to study. Eventually a suitable dish would be selected, and ingredients written down with the Croatian words alongside.

This was a good way of learning vocabulary, but if I could buy 10 per cent of my list I was doing well. It was neither the era nor the place for food that travelled round the world to reach our every whim. Hard currency for imports was scarce, supermarkets were basic, and the real shopping took place in the market, supplied by local producers. Fruit and vegetables came and went with short seasons. Fish stalls were not worth visiting the day after a storm. Lamb before spring was out of the question.

I eventually got the hang of this new survival … shop first, plan second. I became a bit like the Russians who carry a 'lucky bag' made of string netting rolled up in a pocket just in case they get lucky and find something good to buy. Build upon the strength of the best that's available, it's good for you!

This same philosophy is applied by Peter Jackson, Chef Patron and owner of Maes y Neuadd, near Harlech. Beyond the hanging baskets and flower beds there is an idyllic walled garden and orchard, where two full-time gardeners work their magic. The 149 items of fruit and veg only just fit onto a sheet of closely-typed A4.

Each morning, the head gardener reports to the kitchen with the complete list of produce indicating what's at its best. Armed with this knowledge, the chef finalises the day's menu, taking account of any other windfalls: maybe a diver has provided some scallops, a salmon has been caught overnight, wild mushrooms have been picked in the woods at dawn.

Walking back with the marked list, the gardeners set about the

Master chef in his cabbage patch
Photo: Maes y Neuadd Photo Library

daily harvest. At the height of the season it takes the pair of them half a day to deliver the fresh produce all of fifty yards to the kitchen. Any fresher and it would still be growing.

Between them they pick 8 tonnes a year, and fortunately the times of greatest availability coincide with peaks of customer demand. Greenhouses, cold frames and discreetly tucked-away polytunnels lengthen the growing seasons.

I was surprised to find a comprehensive irrigation system in the vegetable garden. Surely with all that moist Atlantic air rising over the Rhinogydd there would be sufficient water? The gardeners explained that it was a feast or famine situation. To cope with frequent torrential downpours the ground is exceedingly porous, and within a relatively short while of the clouds clearing the garden is ready to be worked again. The corollary is that given three days without rain it is like a parched desert and without watering the crops will wither away.

Peter stressed that this was a Welsh Country Hotel as distinct from a Country Hotel in Wales. Wherever possible everything you consume is Welsh, including the lamb from the fields above. This way the customers get optimum freshness, and of course a truly local experience.

The vegetable garden is not just a culinary feast, but an aesthetic inspiration. What better than an early evening stroll in the garden spotting the gaps from where tonight's supper was plucked? Maybe some helpful hints and tips from one of the gardeners?

The restaurant and its chefs have the rosettes and accolades you'd expect but for me the greatest and most visible reassurance of good food is the wonderful backdrop of well-tended fruit and vegetable gardens: you just know it's going to taste great.

Fellow guests and diners will include gourmets and keen gardeners and the occasional celebrity. Senator Edward Kennedy and Jackie Onassis stayed here for the funeral of Lord Harlech, and Sean Connery and Richard Gere made it their base in the filming of *First Knight*.

Needless to say peelings from the kitchen are returned to the soil via the compost heaps. In all probability this practice has been going on since the first people lived here in the fourteenth century … no wonder the soil is so good. Maybe the atmosphere is that bit purer too, with the cooks and gardeners working in tandem to minimise carbon emissions and maximise that tasty local experience – a virtuous circle increasing the odds on survival.

Feast of fish

With coast to the north, west and south of Wales, there's plenty of raw material to hand. It's local, fresh and good for us, but are we doing enough with our seafood?

To make tourism operators more aware of what's available and how to prepare it, Dudley Newbury, the Welsh TV chef, was invited to fire up a group of chefs with some of his passion for using local food in the right season.

Feast was probably the wrong word. The food was wonderful but the minute portions were tantalising, teasing you to crave more. After each dish was prepared it was laid out on a dining plate, photographed and then divided into twenty five tasting portions. Unlike the feeding of the five thousand, these fish had not been blessed.

The local mussel harvest is in full swing during the winter months and the best are to be had from around Bangor and Conwy. A good mussel is a decent size and feels heavy, none of those dainty, flimsy things clinging to rocks at low tide. What you need are shells permanently under water that can feed non-stop. They say the bluer shells are better or sweeter than those in the greyer shells which explains why the Welsh name for mussels is cregyn gleision (blue shells).

Mussels have been harvested at Conwy for hundreds of years. They used to be squashed, the pearls extracted and the meat fed to chickens! *Oeufs mariniére?*

Dudley 'sweated off' the chopped onions to caramelise and reveal their natural sweetness, likewise the mushrooms, which can be very bland until the moisture is removed. Dry cider was added and 'reduced' and as the volume goes down, the intensity of the flavour goes up. At the last minute in went the mussels, herbs and saffron and moments later I was enjoying a taster. Will *'bendigedig'* ever have the same international culinary connotation as *'magnifique'*?

The Welsh name for sea bass is draenogyn môr (*'hedgehog of the sea'*), a reminder not to get in the way of their sharp fins. The local season is from May to November but due to mild winters the fish are still being caught in February, which is one of the upsides to global warming.

Dudley served them stuffed with a mix of garlic, ginger, onion, breadcrumbs, parsley, coriander, lemon zest and chopped prawns, cooked in foil and served with a spicy salsa. This really got my taste buds into overdrive.

Not only did we have Dudley, we also had Gill, of Gill's Plaice. She supplies restaurants and shops with fish landed at Aberdyfi and her role on the day was to explain what was available when, and how to shell, skin or fillet.

She began with a fresh brown crab, twisting off its claws and pushing the body out of the shell. Dead men's fingers were extracted, the stomach sac set aside and

Seabass: draenogyn môr in Welsh or 'hedgehog of the sea'

brown meat was scooped out of the shell. The poorer white meat was taken from the honeycomb and the better stuff separated from the cartilage in the legs and claws. All was neatly packed back into the rinsed out shell converting a £1-60 crab into a £3-50 dressed crab.

Dudley looked across to the finished item and said, 'Some people put mayonnaise on that.' This comment was made with a curled lip in a similar tone to Huw Edwards announcing a particularly evil crime on the 10 o'clock news.

But not crab salad today, instead crab cakes: cooked onions, green beans, breadcrumbs, parsley, roasted almonds, cayenne, paprika, mayonnaise and egg yolk mixed in with the crab and fried in hot groundnut oil.

Next up was monkfish medallions with a summer risotto. The monkfish is generally sold headless to avoid putting one off with its ugly appearance. It is one of the easiest of fish to prepare, no bones but a single cartilage running down the middle.

As for the risotto we wanted lots of vibrant, fresh greens to give it the look of summer. Courgettes were cut lengthways with the seeds scooped out so that the soggy middle would not detract from the crunchy green exterior. Fresh peas were shelled. Asparagus, mange tout and sugar snap peas were sliced lengthways at an angle aiming for similar sizes to allow for even cooking.

Dudley didn't translate *al dente* into Welsh, but it certainly was. Before letting it go too far the fresh cream and parmigiano were added. No matter how enthusiastic you are about local produce, don't be tempted to add Welsh cheddar as a substitute – it's too fatty and won't work.

For people with a phobia about fish bones, fillets are the solution. Gill demonstrated how to fillet a turbot. They grow so big off our coastline they're often referred to as 'dustbin lids' but beware: this is one of the most expensive fish. They are caught on the flat beds where they bury themselves in the sand and pounce on their prey. Lemon sole, on the other hand, are much smaller, cheaper and more fiddly to prepare.

Dudley instructed us in the art of steaming. The slight fillets of lemon sole were rolled up into little taste bombs with a core of salsa in the middle, wrapped in cling film twisted at each end and tied together. A line of crab cake mix was run lengthways along a turbot fillet and folded over. Once in the cling film it looked like a fat white sausage, ideal for preparing ahead and leaving in the fridge. Served with a hot salsa I thought I was in heaven.

I asked Dudley what would success look like? What would be an indicator that Wales had got its act together on food?

He said more food programmes on TV, but then again I suppose you'd expect a TV chef to say that. 'Greater emphasis on education, not into the technology but into the basics of preparing good food. Maybe Wales getting its third Michelin star? Compared to Scotland with twelve stars, we've got some catching up to do.'

In the meantime it's crazy to see Canadian lobsters in our supermarket freezers, whilst wonderful fresh specimens landed at Barmouth and other harbours are exported via Holyhead to Spain! Fellow Celts in Brittany wouldn't let this happen: why should we?

Porth Meudwy, where pilgrims used to – and still do – embark for Bardsey (Ynys Enlli), is a case which gives hope for the future. With the help of European funding and farm buildings from the National Trust the port has been upgraded with safe landing, cold storage, ice making and fish processing facilities. This means the six part-time fishermen can add value and create more money from the finite number of crabs and lobsters that this part of the coast can sustain – so much better to create a local experience than export raw materials to a distant chef.

Rural Crafts

Progress can be a great thing and each generation leaves its mark on the landscape, be it an enduring feature or an improved rural skill. Recent generations have had the 'benefit' of ready-made, mass-produced goods as opposed to using natural raw materials, and in pursuit of greater efficiency or convenience these have supplanted the traditional. The legacy is miles of rusty fencing, characterless structures of galvanised iron and disposable barbecues with charcoal from far away.

The age of cheap energy for manufacture and transport with unsustainable levels of pollution is over and it's not a moment too soon, before we completely forget how to make things ourselves. Obviously there needs to be a balance between what's practical and what's economically viable, but wherever possible the DIY sustainable approach should be preferred. These skills are important, not just to keep alive our heritage and hundreds of years of accumulated know-how, but to reconnect us with the reality of the countryside in a hands-on way as opposed to what is increasingly experienced second-hand through the medium of television.

Woven hurdles

Woven hurdles have been used by farmers for centuries, the instant barrier to create a pen, block a gateway or provide shelter to animals. Sadly this sustainable method has gone the way of many rural crafts and been replaced by lightweight aluminium barriers.

But there are still a few people who know how to make hurdles, albeit the applications have changed. Instead of portable hurdles for farmers, the vast majority of the market is for fixed hurdles in gardens as windbreaks or attractive natural fences. These days they need to be able to withstand rampant sweet peas as opposed to determined sheep.

In the past, owners of large farms would create and manage woodland areas so they could be self-sufficient with the raw materials. On a rotation basis the woodland would be 'coppiced', a posh word for 'cut' which is said to derive from the French verb 'couper'. I know a lecturer at Plas Tan y Bwlch (the national park's training centre) who says coppice derives from 'coed pys', the Welsh for 'pea sticks', but I think he might be winding me up.

A coppiced woodland would include a mix of hazel, willow, chestnut and ash, each having its particular uses, but for hurdling, hazel is the prime material. Large trees would be spaced far enough apart to create the ideal environment for the hazel to grow underneath, nice and straight towards the canopy – straight wood is so much easier to work with.

The great thing about coppicing is that it goes on forever: cut it back and it sprouts again. The frequency with which to coppice depends on the job intended, but every seven to twelve years would be the norm – any longer and the hazel rods would be too thick to work with. These days, the best hazel woodlands are to be found in south-east England.

I was lucky to take part in a hurdle-making course arranged by Meirionnydd Oakwoods, an EU-funded project to regenerate and conserve the Atlantic oakwoods. Atlantic oakwoods – so called because they are on the edge of the Atlantic and bathed in the warm and moist air from the gulf-stream which provides a unique growing environment. The European coast from Scotland to Portugal used to be covered in such woods but today there is very little left and the best that survives is in Meirionnydd.

The big picture is to salvage and conserve these oakwoods. This is not a one-off chain saw job cutting out conifers and revealing ancient oaks – there's a whole lot more. One aspect is to shift our understanding and perception, to turn the clock back and get people into the woods, not just for picnics and walks, but also to work

Trimming hazel on a shaving horse

the woods and practice the woodland crafts such as making charcoal, besoms (witches' brooms) and hurdles.

We drove to some woods where recent forestry works had revealed a couple of ornamental ponds from Victorian times, with stunning views across the Mawddach Estuary. Our job was to create some hurdles beside the ponds as a backdrop for a picnic area.

The two basic types of hurdle are 'wattle', which forms a complete screen and thus provides protection from the weather ideal for baby lambs, and 'riven', which looks like a rustic portable five-bar gate, stronger and good for restraining cattle.

The wattle design seemed more relevant to our picnickers, and bearing in mind our hurdles would not be portable, we would build them big and use substantial timbers at the top and bottom. For these we scavenged some birch tree trunks about 3 or 4 inches thick, and cut them into 6 foot lengths. These were then drilled with five equidistant holes of 1 inch diameter. The purist would have used a brace and bit but a cordless power drill was a convenient alternative.

Meanwhile, the straightest bits of hazel we could find were cut into 6 foot poles and pointed. The poles were clamped in a shaving horse, an ingenious gadget that grips the timber whilst leaving both hands free to use a draw knife and neatly trim the ends. Once the right diameter was achieved these were then refined with a round planer, a bit like a giant's pencil sharpener, to create a perfect cylinder of wood to fit the holes drilled in the birch, and thus make a strong joint.

Five lengths of hazel were slotted upright into the bottom length of birch, and the crossbar piece was attached at the top. This required a little bit of encouragement from the rustic hammer, a lump of wood with a handle carved at one end. It's the perfect woodland tool, free and easy to make, and when it breaks you've got a log for your fire.

The frame was then put in place attached to an oak post at either end, and the weaving began, using whatever we could find lying on the ground. Old conifer worked well, birch was a bit brittle, rhododendron was OK – if only ponticum could grow as straight as hazel maybe someone would love it. These were threaded between the five upright hazels, putting the thick end in from alternate directions.

It was beginning to look like a woven hurdle, but the design included a window (for bird-watching) which meant the threads would not have the pressure of five uprights to keep them in place. For these more challenging sections we used freshly-cut willow stems, which were flexible enough to be wound round the poles.

Once the hurdle was fully woven we secured it to the posts, making sure it was clear of the ground as keeping the hurdle out of the wet earth gives it a much longer life. The loose ends were trimmed off and a few stems of willow planted at the base to give it a life of its own.

You can buy a woven hurdle from a garden centre, £68 should get you a 6 foot square hurdle, but it's much more fun to build your own. I've since built my own shaving horse and added a draw knife and round planer to my collection of tools, and each time I walk in the woods I have a much keener eye for the types and shapes of wood.

Charcoal – a burning issue

In developing countries, charcoal is at the core of life: for most people it is the only way of cooking or heating. Of course, it is possible to burn wood, but it generates less heat, more smoke, and is much heavier to handle. Seven tonnes of wood converts into one tonne of charcoal, and if you've got to carry it several miles on your back the energy savings are plain to see or be felt.

For thousands of years charcoal was a key part of life and employment in Britain. It was the only way to generate the high temperatures (1500° C) necessary for smelting bronze and iron.

Large-scale smelting of iron ore was a roving industry based on the availability of ore and a suitable supply of trees. In the early eighteenth century, Abraham Darby worked briefly in Dolgellau helping to establish the Dolgun smelting furnace. For three and a half years they did nothing but fell trees and convert them to charcoal. Having laid up a huge stockpile of charcoal, the furnace was lit and burnt for forty weeks, converting iron ore into iron until the supply of charcoal was exhausted and the furnace was closed. Abraham Darby subsequently went on to become famous as the man who pioneered the use of coke in a blast furnace process for smelting iron. Thereafter, production moved to permanent sites based on the great coalfields of south Wales, Flintshire and elsewhere – a major leap forward in the industrial revolution, but the death knell for Britain's charcoal industry.

Today's applications for charcoal include gunpowder, art, compost and filtration, but by far the greatest volume is what we burn on our barbecues.

Sadly, over 90 per cent of what we consume is imported, and even sadder still, much of that comes from unsustainable sources that should be protected, such as the mangrove forests in Indonesia. You can tell mangrove charcoal by its weight, much heavier and denser than British charcoal and most likely to take hours to set alight. Mangrove charcoal has 60 per cent carbon content, whereas British charcoal has about 85 per cent, which means it is very good at producing a lot of heat and when you want it – no need for lighter fuel to get it going and taint the food.

Britain is a great place to make charcoal of good quality with minimal environmental impact whilst creating rural employment and encouraging better woodland management. True, it is a bit of a messy job, but nothing that won't come out in the wash. In the best of all possible worlds charcoal will be made in woodland that needs managing anyway, and transported a minimal distance to the nearest retail outlet – i.e. it should be done locally, and therefore on a small scale.

Making charcoal is a smoky business but nothing that won't come out in the wash

To this end, I put my name down for a charcoal course in Coed y Brenin, part of the great Atlantic Oakwoods north of Dolgellau.

The raw ingredients are relatively small pieces of hardwood trees that would otherwise go to waste. Best quality comes from alder, oak and beech. Sycamore, birch, willow and poplar can also be used, and typically there will be a mix in a given bag.

The key tool is a ring kiln, a heavy duty cylinder of iron with a conical lid, about 6 feet in diameter and 4 feet tall set on a series of ventilation spigots. The kiln is stacked with logs of up to 6 inches in diameter and lit. The first half hour is the most impressive with dense emissions of mainly steam spewing out. As the steam switches to smoke, the input of air is reduced and confined to three or four chimneys that are put in place. It's then a matter of waiting between eighteen to twenty-six hours until the logs have been converted to charcoal. A bit like waiting for the election of a new pope, but what you are looking for is thin, blue and wispy smoke.

Once complete the chimneys are removed, the air supply is completely cut off, and the whole thing left for at least twenty-four hours. Premature opening and the whole thing will go up in flames!

Emptying the kiln involved the most amazing Heath Robinson contraption. A home made rotating cage mounted on bicycle wheels and driven by a battery-powered windscreen-wiper motor. The charcoal rolls down the cage into sacks at the far end with dust and small bits filtered off on the way – these fragments are useful for mixing in to compost.

Our instructor talked us through the marketing and distribution of small-scale charcoal production. Most of his own production is sold and delivered direct to local stores of B&Q: he is part of a network of producers around the country co-ordinated through a focal point to supply this customer. Networking and co-operative working are key aspects to accessing the big customers and making this activity financially fruitful.

That said, this is not a get-rich-quick option, but then again, neither is preserving ancient woodland. The rewards are modest, with each 'burn' of a 6 foot kiln producing about 150 kilos of saleable charcoal, which, at a minimum trade price of £0.80 per kilo, makes £120 before consumable costs such as bags and fuel. But when added in to a related activity, it can make a profitable sideline, as well as being environmentally friendly and keeping things local and rural.

Back at home I explained to my son the theory of making charcoal and together we improvised an old galvanised bin into a kiln, filled it, lit it and supposedly sealed it. Much smoke and a few hours later we had a pile of ashes for our efforts – but even if we're no good at making it, we are committed to the principle of burning local.

Hedge laying – and dormice?

I booked myself onto this course because I was keen to learn how to lay a hedge and curious to know what dormice had to do with the subject!

Rhodri, from the National Trust at Ganllwyd, introduced us to the basics of laying a hedge using an overgrown one that had not been laid since the conifers were planted in the 1930s. In those days this hedge would have been used to restrain stock, but our purposes were more to do with conservation and aesthetics.

The old line of the hedge could still be made out by a row of mature hazel trees, albeit with large gaps between. We started at the top end, because hedges are laid uphill as this is the direction in which trees grow. We took out the dead wood and removed the large branches and trunks that were pointing in the wrong direction.

One by one the branches were bent up the line of the hedge and using a billhook, the bottom end, about 3 inches off the ground, was cut into until it could be 'laid' at an angle of about 30° to the woodland floor – the important thing being to retain a sufficient core of the branch and its bark to form a hinge so that life can flow from the roots.

Stakes were driven into the ground every 2 feet or so through which the laid branches were twisted, thereby giving it strength and a straight line.

Quite simple really but in putting theory into practice several things did not go quite to plan, such as the branches snapping off. Also, because the hedge had not been maintained for so many years there were several gaps that had to be filled with cut branches, and these were supplemented with freshly cut sticks of willow. Put a piece of thin, freshly cut willow into the ground and it will have a 99 per cent success rate of rooting and growing into a tree.

Our other tutor was Jack, a veteran of dormice conservation. Dormice numbers have fallen dramatically in recent years and this is thought to be a consequence of the disappearing hedgerows and ancient woodlands.

The newly-laid hedge would be a vital corridor for these tiny creatures that spend almost all of their life off the ground to avoid the predators that lurk below. Without corridors it is difficult for dormice to move to other areas, limiting their ability to feed and to breed with neighbouring communities.

Jack's spin on hedge-laying was not only to create the corridor, but also to retain the built-in food supply. It takes seven years or more before hazel branches mature and produce nuts, so we went out of our way to make sure we retained and made good use of the fruit bearing branches.

Having laid a section of hedge we turned our attention to a large area recently cleared of conifers – treeless ground is a dormice desert. With mattocks, spades

Sleeping through the midwinter check-up.
Photo: Rhian Hughes, North Wales Wildlife Trust

and sacks full of hazel saplings we set about planting in a random fashion in contrast with the regimented lines used for densely packed sitka spruce plantations. Not only are straight lines unnatural, they also make it that much easier for goats or deer to wreak havoc with your regeneration plans.

As with any course held in the woods of Snowdonia, there is a distinct possibility of rain, and this day was to be no exception when it came with a driving certainty. Fortunately Jack had erected a makeshift shelter, and we huddled under it for sandwiches whilst he told us more about these rarely-seen creatures. Being nocturnal, in the trees and asleep for up to three quarters of their life, there's little chance of bumping into one.

The key giveaway that dormice are about is the presence of hazelnut shells. They eat about fourteen nuts a night taking approximately 20 minutes with each one – it's quite an effort for a small creature to break into the tough shells. They leave a distinctive pattern and Jack showed us how to differentiate between these and nuts opened by wood mice, squirrels, bank voles and nuthatches.

The presence of shells will tell you they've been around but it could have been ages ago. Through practice and research Jack has devised a sophisticated system of age-grading from '*impossible to break between thumb and fingers*' being last autumn, to '*easily squidged with a splat*' being five years or more. Varying degrees of facial expressions, grunts and adjectives define the ages in between.

A lot of people have been granted licenses to take part in dormice monitoring schemes based on putting up and regularly checking nesting boxes. Jack took us through the practicalities – how to safely extract without injuring or losing them, how to weigh them, how to mark and put them back into their box.

At a low level this is relatively easy but there's also a lot of activity higher up in the tree canopy which complicates things. The logistics of siting and inspecting a box 25 feet up a conifer are quite challenging – if you've ever tried to climb one you'll appreciate that conifers are not easy. A ladder might help but is a heavy object to carry around the woods and health and safety regulations would expect a second person to hold the base steady. Another problem is to reach the box without scaring the creatures into running away.

Being clever and full of 'high' tech ideas, Jack has invented the pole box based on a tall pole, from 15 to 25 feet long, on which the box is mounted. The poles are made from straight, thin conifers, preferably left a season to dry out, thereby being light and easy to manoeuvre.

Attached to the top of the pole is the nesting box made from a piece of drain pipe with wooden discs to block the top and bottom. An entrance hole is cut into the pipe, and the outside surface scored with a soldering iron to provide grip and make it climbable. A piece of rubber from an old tyre tube is used to hold the box together.

In the early prototype days Jack would lower the pole and find plenty of evidence of nesting materials but was unable to inspect without the dormice fleeing. This problem was overcome with a shutter made from an outer ring of drain pipe cut vertically so that it was still a tight fit but could be moved up and down by pulling a length of string running down the pole through staples.

I had always thought conifer plantations to be wildlife deserts, but based on this high but low technology Jack now has concrete proof of this endangered species surviving way up in the canopy of conifers. Who knows, maybe in years to come children will be told the tale of Jack and the Pole Box.

Who built the stone walls?

Driving west towards Snowdonia, brick gives way to stone, rolling hills to craggy cliffs, and hedgerows are replaced with dry stone walls. I love these walls, they are like an ancient signature on the land.

My house is 500 years old, but the rocks of which it is built are a million times older. Just outside the front door a retaining wall holds up the opposite bank and at its base is one of my favourites. All sorts of colours including red, yellow and orange intermingle with the grey and brown, and embedded in its heart is a fossil-like shape. Showing a visitor around I suggested it might even be a dinosaur ankle.

I hadn't realised she was a geology boffin and she quickly dissed my theory, 'These rocks were here at least three hundred million years before dinosaurs came into existence! But it might be a fossilised fern'.

I was disappointed although the rest of the impromptu lecture was every bit as exciting. Our underlying geology is a mix of sedimentary and volcanic rocks formed during eruptions under the sea 500 million years ago. As the earth's plates

The Snowdonia Society's annual stone walling competition

collided 350 million years or more ago, these rocks were pushed up into the massive mountains of Snowdonia and subsequently sculpted by the weather, and melting glaciers in particular.

As for the dates of all these stone walls, you don't need a geologist but a historian. A small proportion date back to medieval or pre-historic farming, and these tend to be rather higgledy piggledy, boundaries for small areas. But the vast majority date back to the early 1800s and these are much more 'Victorian', defiant of nature, running in bold straight lines up the steepest mountains and following high contour lines to separate the 'ffridd' from the wilder mountain tops. 'Ffridd' is a great word to describe the land between upland and lowland, typically with lots of rocks and bracken and a mosaic of pasture or woodland.

Britain's population quadrupled to 18 million between the start and end of the eighteenth century, on the back of the industrial revolution, placing huge demands on the use of land for food production. The demand for higher productivity led to The Enclosure Acts, which took land out of common and into private ownership, with anyone else on the land becoming a tenant or being evicted. In Wales the enclosures began in the lowlands in the 1500s and the uplands from about 1750 onwards. This was boom time for stone-wallers.

It also coincided with the end of the Napoleonic Wars at Waterloo in 1815, at which point there were a million people in Britain's armed forces. Stone-walling was a massive job creation scheme for the returning soldiers, but after fifteen years of serving King and country it must have felt like short change to be posted up a wet and windy mountain in winter.

Walls are highly functional, enduring and ideally suited to the landscape. The raw materials are plentiful and ready to hand and sometimes the stones are the by-product of land improvement, extracted to improve the pasture for rough haymaking and to prevent scythes being blunted. They survive the worst of weathers and also provide protection for livestock as they huddle in on the leeward side, particularly useful at lambing time.

Not only are they good to look at and useful for controlling livestock, they're also an important wildlife corridor teeming with creatures such as field voles and their never-far-away predators, stoats and weasels, which use the walls as homes and vantage points from which to pinpoint their next meal.

I've repaired lots of walls around my house. The roots of a huge tree growing from the base of a wall had destabilised the foundations, so I built a by-pass around it with enough space for the trunk to rock in the wind. The edge of a gateway had been clipped by the tractor (it had been built with single horsepower in mind), so I brought it up to date, making it a bit wider.

Walls will not endure indefinitely without maintenance, and a poorly placed stone will eventually start to rock in the constant battering of the wind, or be squeezed out as ice forms and thaws. A falling branch, or people and animals climbing over them, will dislodge a stone. A small breach in the wall is the thin end of the wedge: once word gets around that this is a good crossing point it's not long before the trickle has become a torrent and it's no longer stock-proof. A stone in time saves nine?

My technique is self-taught from books and mistakes and the joy of mucking around with rough building blocks. But there is always room for improvement, so I joined in a walling course in the woods at Coed Felenrhyd above Maentwrog.

This wall was more than just an academic exercise – the Woodland Trust wanted it repaired so they could re-introduce sheep grazing in a controlled way to keep down the brambles and ivy that were in danger of choking out other plantlife, such as rare lichens.

After the health and safety briefing we cleared the fallen wall, creating long piles of easy-to-reach stone on either side of the base. Our instructor drove in a pair of stakes at either end, attaching pieces of wood to make a tapered A shape with string running either side from the stakes at one end to those at the other. Large stones were placed at the base butting on to the line, with smaller stones or 'hearting' filling the gaps in the middle. As the structure rose out of the ground the line was moved up and the wall became a bit thinner. Through-stones, running through from one side to the other, were placed every so often to bind the wall together, and large stones on the top to hold things in place. By way of decoration it was crowned with moss to make our new work blend in with the 200 year-old section adjoining.

There is something inherently pleasing about dry stone walls, not forced to co-exist with mortar, but living in a balance of natural forces. Stones are timeless and re-usable building blocks of the countryside and, whilst you don't need to be strong or an expert to have a go, there are many fantastic examples both old and new that are testament to a craft which is alive and well in Snowdonia.

Community

Many of the great things in Snowdonia have survived by chance or lack of intervention. They are still there because they have not been demolished in urban development or because the ground was too rocky for deep ploughing or the various species were perfectly suited to our temperate climate.

Other things are kept alive through the passion and spirit of the people that live here. Maybe a village, a school or a language, but the really important survivor is the sense of community that brings people together. As our society becomes increasingly transient and multi-ethnic these will be challenging times for communities.

Croesor – community café at the foot of the 'Welsh Matterhorn'

Croesor is a small village in a glacial valley overlooked by the sharp peak of Cnicht. From behind, the mountain top looks like a knight wearing a helmet, and some people think this is how Cnicht got its name, from an old English word. But this is highly unlikely in such a bastion of Welshness. More likely the name derives from the Gaelic word which means pointed hill. Looking up from the west, the mountain is a perfectly formed peak sometimes referred to as the 'Welsh Matterhorn'.

During Victorian times the valley was a busy place with miners quarrying into the side of Moelwyn Mawr. Slates were transported by mule across the mountain to the Ffestiniog Railway. Later a horse-drawn tramway was constructed to converge with the Welsh Highland Railway and thence to ships at Porthmadog.

The village is home to thirty residents and is the 'centre' for a few outlying farms. It used to have a school, which was built by the quarrymen, and which in recent years had clung on to an exclusive existence with fewer than ten pupils.

Access is by single-track road past Plas Brondanw, the old family home of Clough Williams-Ellis, the architect and creator of Portmeirion.

Croesor lost its Post Office and village shop in the 1960s, but when a man from the Midlands announced he was going to convert a derelict farm into self-catering chalets the villagers were spurred into action to safeguard the character of their community. Instead of an absentee landlord or part-time resident they wanted something more permanent: something that added to, rather than diluted, the unique flavour of the community and its heritage, something that provided employment and a focal point for village life.

There was much discussion about what should be done, about what makes Croesor so special and what are its natural assets.

Looking up from the village the answer lies in the wild landscape and inspiring range of mountains that draws walkers from miles away. The car park is often full and a testimony to the popularity of the nearby peaks. The shame and the opportunity is that they come and go throughout the year without stopping to enjoy the village itself.

To redress this, the villagers decided to convert the old Bryngelynnen Farm into a centre for both the walkers and the community. In the first phase, a beautiful café has been created where you can relax beside an inglenook fireplace with a slice of home-made cake served by any one of the nineteen volunteers trained up in food hygiene. The café has been tastefully restored using conventional materials,

Croesor Caffi beneath Cnicht

and won the 2007 Rural Award from CPRW – The Campaign for the Preservation of Rural Wales (Meirionnydd branch).

A further award was presented for traditional slate fencing which beckons people along the path from the car park to indulge themselves in the café. These formidable slabs of slate have been buried deep in the ground to keep them upright and straight, and are a good use of local resources.

In the second phase one part of the building has been converted into a gallery for local artists, and in the third phase the ramshackle barn will be converted into a stylish bunkhouse for up to twenty walkers. To help it blend into the landscape the bunkhouse roof will be covered with turf and thus it will be invisible to people up the mountain. It is intended to use this as a venue for residential training courses in subjects such as rural crafts.

Grants are available for this sort of project, but half the money needed to be matched and raised by the village, and to this end they opened Siop Mela, a charity shop in the nearby town of Penrhyndeudraeth, staffed, of course, by volunteers. Several years on, the shop continues to be a great success and much appreciated by all who use it.

It just goes to show what can be achieved with commitment and determination. The village has a long tradition of community projects, which includes the building of an open-air swimming pool filled with crystal clear water running off the mountain. The pool is built into the natural rocks and allows for disabled access, not to mention the occasional brown trout. What better way to end a day's walking than a few lengths of backstroke looking up at Cnicht, followed by coffee and cake at the café.

Better still if the cake has been cooked in the communal bread oven built in the garden – it's a dome of cob, set on old storage heater bricks. Cob is a combination of clay, sand, straw and water paddled together by the villagers with their trousers rolled up, a bit like trampling the grapes, and applied in three layers. At weekends and on special occasions the oven is lit and everyone is welcome to bring along their dough – when the fire is scooped out pizzas go in first to make use of the fiercest heat and as the temperature subsides the bread, then the cakes and casseroles take their turn. It puts a new dimension on the term 'village bakery'.

In the middle of the village is a small rockery with engraved standing stones. Each stone represents an era in the life of the village, covering Roman times, early agriculture, slate quarrying, the progress of the school and so on. What I really like about Croesor is the strong spirit of community as it downsizes and reforms, but I'm not quite sure how that should be carved onto a piece of slate.

Islands in the lake

Trawsfynydd means 'across the mountain' derived from the latin *'trans mons'* and reflects its historically significant location. A Bronze Age trackway runs through Traws, as locals call it, with the track rising from the coast into the hills above Harlech passing numerous standing stones and thought to have been the ancient route from Ireland to Stonehenge.

Traws is a small town of just under a thousand people, and has had a series of disproportionately large employers over the centuries, stretching back to Roman times with the fort, Tomen y Mur. This subsequently became the site of a Norman motte and bailey castle and, in the late nineteenth century, rail access and remote countryside made nearby Bronaber an ideal location for an artillery training camp.

In the 1970s and 1980s much of Wales' electricity was generated here from Britain's only inland nuclear power station. When it was generating it worked round the clock with a staff of 420 spread across the shifts, and during the decommissioning phase there have been about 500 workers on site.

The Camelot scene in *First Knight* was filmed here with a mock castle constructed on one of the islands and computer-generated graphics superimposed on the reactor buildings

But in a couple of years, when the reactor buildings are lowered, the bulk of the work will be complete and there will be but a few care and maintenance jobs.

The loss of jobs will undoubtedly be a big blow but the community is both determined and suitably experienced to survive the change. The local regeneration company is called Trawsnewid, with 'newid' being the verb 'to change'.

To remind the community of its past and boost its appeal to tourists Trawsnewid has created an excellent interpretation centre in the village. As well as good overnight accommodation you can learn about the local hero Hedd Wynn, who was posthumously awarded the bardic chair at the 1917 Eisteddfod, having died on the battlefields of Flanders, and Saint John Roberts the martyr, famous for the work he did for sufferers during the Great Plague and executed in 1610 for high treason, i.e. practising his Catholic beliefs.

The most distinctive feature of the local landscape is Llyn Trawsfynydd. At the shallow end there is a long footbridge connecting outlying farms with the town – when the dam wall was built for the hydro-electric scheme, and the level of the lake raised in the 1920s, farmers were offered the choice between a bridge and free electricity for life.

The lake is a haven for fish and one of the four venues on which the national fishing trials are held. Apart from those with rods there are others interested in the fishing and these include otters, mink, herons, cormorants and more recently ospreys. Particularly vulnerable are freshly stocked rainbow trout which have no 'lake credibility' when it comes to fending for themselves. There are not many places for them to hide as the shoreline rises and falls with the rain and the amount released for hydro-electricity. At low tide the muddy beach provides no protection whatsoever.

To provide a safe refuge five eco-islands have been installed at a cost of £40,000 between the bridge and where the Afon Prysor flows in to the lake. Submerged beneath the surface are large cages into which otters and cormorants are unable to chase the fish.

But these islands have many more uses. Sprouting out from the top is a mix of reeds and other aquatic plants that act as natural filters and reduce the build up of algal bloom. This is not an attractive pond plant but a build up of algae and bacteria that sucks out the oxygen and turns the water into the colour and consistency of pea soup. It can occur naturally, for example through leaves falling and decomposing in the water, but the primary cause is the leaching of nitrates and phosphates into the river, typically from the application of fertiliser. The problem is compounded by the build up of silt and in shallow waters where the temperature is raised by the rays of the sun.

The good thing about the reeds is they are hungry for nitrogen phosphate and suck it out of the water. They also provide a sunshade keeping the waters below cooler. For maximum effect these 'floating reedbeds' have been placed along the channel where the river enters the lake.

The islands serve as life-

Hedd Wynn at dawn

rafts for dragonflies and other insects which can thrive in the clean water. The better the insect life, the better the fish and the fishing. Likewise more insects will mean more birds, and some species will take advantage of safe nesting sites. Newts and other amphibians benefit too.

One of the intentions is to create a mid-way haven between the RSPB reserves at Conwy and Ynys Hir, near Machynlleth, thereby creating a north Wales corridor of bird activity. In particular it is hoped to attract the bittern, a bird that relies on reedbed habitat and with less than fifty pairs in Britain, they really get the twitchers excited.

More fish, more birds, more eco-tourism, and to make it easier the car park is being upgraded and disabled access facilities provided to make the wildlife and landscape open to all. A viewing hide will be erected and an interpretation board will explain what's here.

And for those seeking a bit of luxury, guided tours on board an Amsterdam canal cruiser are an option. This boat was buried during World War II, covered in sand along with other boats in a drained section of canal, and thus kept safely from the occupying German army. For many years it saw service on Lake Windermere before undergoing a thorough refurbishment, getting a new mooring on Llyn Trawsfynydd and being renamed MV Prysorwen.

'Around the Lake in 80 Minutes'? Now that would make a great film.

Cymraeg – if not now, then when?

I think our language is great. Travel to Wales and there is no mistaking you are abroad – this is not a 'region', but a country, with all the culture, history and independent way of thinking that goes with it. Visitors can really feel like foreigners (welcome, of course) particularly in Snowdonia, one of the areas where Welsh is, and always has been, the dominant language.

Cymraeg is an ancient language, Celtic in origin, influenced by the Romans, and has taken many knocks over the centuries. In the last hundred years our population has almost doubled to three million but the proportion of Welsh speakers has more than halved to 22 percent. Since the Welsh Language Act of 1993 the decline has been reversed from a 19 per cent low.

Language decline is happening all over the world with many becoming extinct. Death of a language is like losing a species of bird or plant. In January 2008 Eyak, one of the twenty languages in Alaska, passed away almost unnoticed with the death of the last speaker.

The main threat is a killer language, and Cymraeg sits next door to the birthplace of the greatest killer of all, Saesneg (English). It's become a dominant medium for communication, with technology making it ever more widespread.

The embodiment and future of Cymraeg lies in the community of mother-tongue (mam-iaith) speakers. But learners can do their bit as well. If not me, then who? If not now, then when?

My excuses are many. One of the perennials is, 'I'm too old, it's all very well for young kids, that's the time to learn etc.' but the reality is that when young children learn Welsh they put in more effort. In Snowdonia there's no escape at school, it's the language of the playground. If you want to fit in and get on, you need to know it. It's not just the advantage of a young mind, it's the application of it – and adults have a habit of being 'too busy'.

No language is easy, and Welsh has features that English speakers don't have to contend with. A big challenge is saying 'yes' or 'no', where the response depends upon the tense or the way the question was asked, a minefield of options that generally confounds learners into a mute nod of the head. On the positive side Welsh is a phonetic language, what you see is what you say, whereas English pronunciation is a nightmare for learners – cough, chough, bough, bought, through, thorough.

Mutations are another stumbling block – if you let them be. 'I live in Maentwrog' but 'I come from Faentwrog'! But that's a whole lot easier than living in Caernarfon, which can mutate to 'yng Nghaernarfon'. To learn the rules is about as mind-numbing as reading a phonebook. It's best approached a bit like a trainee Jedi knight: feel the force, make mistakes and adapt with experience, as a child would. Mutations are helpful friends to make the language sing. English has its own mutations but they are more spoken as opposed to written.

Are we doing enough to secure the future of Cymraeg? Are we making it easier for would-be-speakers?

The creation of S4C in 1982, resulting from Gwynfor Evans's hunger strike in 1980, must rank amongst the most significant achievements and many years on has been developed to provide a steady stream of programmes, not only for the fluent, but for learners too. Now S4C Digidol is available, and exclusively Welsh-language.

Like many other terrestrial broadcasters, S4C's viewing figures have declined dramatically, and advertising revenues, albeit a small fraction of the overall funding, have dropped from a peak of £13m in 2003 to just over £5m. The catalyst for these declines has been the exercise of choice brought about by the digital option. In addition, many viewers can now tune in to Channel 4 rather than watching the same English-language programmes shown on S4C, such as *Big Brother*. In response to this there are calls to increase the number of English-language programmes about Wales.

Radio Cymru has introduced *Pigion,* a news programme covering highlights of the past week, with easy to understand introductions – getting you on board with the basics before steaming off in turbo-Welsh. And just in case you were thinking of an excuse such as it's on at the wrong time, it's available as a podcast so you can enjoy it when you want, as often as you want.

All too often learners like myself are reading or listening to something which is a bit complex and you lose the plot early on, eyes gloss over, and you give up to await rescue. *Lingo Newydd*, the bi-monthly Welsh language magazine for learners, presents the information in a useful way. Each article is laid out in three colours indicating language simplicity. Starting with the blue for novices you can quickly get the gist of a story with unfamiliar words covered in a brief vocabulary beneath. Armed with the outline of the story it's much easier to tackle the intermediate and ultimately the full-blown sections. The magazine helps you build on a simple base, to walk before you run or at least crawl before you walk.

Online courses have been around for a while and have been cumbersome and clunky, another good excuse for not getting on with it. But I've just experienced the *Big Welsh Challenge* on the BBC website and it's brilliant, in a totally different league to what has gone before. On entering the site learners can select between north or south Wales variations. Based on a soap opera it provides high quality education and entertainment with subtitles or speech bubbles to convert spoken into written words.

If not me then who?

At the end of all my study efforts I suspect my grasp will at best be passable, it won't be the rich understanding of everyday spoken Welsh, neither the vernacular spoken by my neighbouring farmers nor the richness of a bard. But my young son will have made that transition and therein lies the hope.

Even though my father had Welsh as his first language, he encouraged us towards French and German as being 'useful and modern'. With hindsight it was a poor choice – I occasionally meet someone from France or Germany but I meet my neighbours everyday.

This great language, with its rich oral and literary depths, has survived against the odds through the spirit and determination of its mam-iaith speakers – many people went to prison for the sake of it. Against a background of greater mobility of people and the ever more pervasive reach of the internet there has never been a more important time to recruit new speakers. It's not a single generation quick fix, but a matter of long-term mindshift and hard graft.

If not now, then when? I can't think of any more excuses for not getting on with it.

Remarkable

There's nothing bland and boring about Snowdonia. It's a place that is significantly different to neighbouring areas and leaves a lasting impression. The rivers flow faster, the mountains rise higher and everywhere you look there are reminders of remarkable stories and characters from the past that survive and endure the test of re-telling, stories that relate the area to national or world events or which lift it out of the humdrum and give it that unforgettable appeal. When you leave a place you take with you a set of memories that anchor it in your mind – for me it is the combination of these remarkable stories against the backdrop of spectacular landscape that will keep Snowdonia alive in my imagination forever.

Wild car

Not a Mustang nor a Ferrari, but a skimpy piece of wood mounted on a wheel and a rod of iron racing 50 mph down a Welsh mountain.

Getting slate down the mountain from the high quarries of Ffestiniog was a feat of Victorian engineering ingenuity. The power was provided by a wagon full of slate going down to pull up an empty wagon on a pair of narrow gauge rails running the length of an incline. In the middle of each track was a steel rope, running on rollers, which connected the dependent wagons.

The Craig Ddu quarry above Manod had a set of three inclines to reach the road, and a fourth to link with the railway below running to Blaenau. This was the route to market. It was also the quickest way home for the workers after a hard day's work.

I asked Emrys Evans, who was apprenticed at the quarry in 1933, how fast cars went down an incline. 'I can't tell you in seconds, but I can describe it as follows. At the end of the shift the men were allowed to place their cars on the track and as soon as the 4 o'clock hooter blasted from the Oakeley quarry, they were off. Most people started from the second incline. They were able to do these two inclines, run between them, put the car into an empty wagon, and reach the bus stop by the time the bus to Blaenau departed 5 minutes later. Buses were very punctual in those days.'

The length of the inclines to the road was 1,800 yards with a descent of 1,040 feet, and the journey, including the connecting sections, was reputedly done in about 8 minutes.

The wild car (car gwyllt) was an innovation credited to the quarry's blacksmith in the 1870s. It ran between the two pairs of rails which were separated by a gap of 3 feet, and, more importantly, without any obstructions such as the rollers between the narrow gauge tracks.

The car consisted of very little. A piece of wood about 2 feet long and 8 inches wide, with a 'flanged' iron wheel towards the front and a V-shaped iron heel at the back. An iron bar stretched out from the centre of the board across to the other track to provide the balance on the other rail. Speed was controlled with a brake, which consisted of a handle between the driver's knees that pressed a brake pad against the wheel – heels were also used!

'There was no driving test as such,' explained Emrys. 'You simply sat on the car, pointed your legs straight out and leaned inwards onto the iron cross bar to get a good balance. The key was to avoid going too fast and losing control. When I first started at the quarry I would follow after the person I was apprenticed to, with my

Rush hour at the quarry

feet pressed into his back. But after a couple of weeks I was going solo.'

At its peak the quarry employed more than 200 workers. Rush hour must have been quite a sight, and fortunately the occasion was captured in *The Quarryman (Y Chwarelwr)* which was filmed in 1934. (Emrys helped with the recent reconstruction of the missing reel of this film.)

Just looking at the inclines and the cars makes one think of danger and accidents, and there were many. Inexperience and recklessness were the main causes and, unlike tobogganing out of control, there was no soft landing from a car gwyllt. A driver's heel extended to slow his descent could kick slate onto the track and derail the car. Leaning too much or too little could cause the car to overbalance, and a stray foot could snag in the tracks. If you survived the impact you still had the risk of a substantial fall over the edge of the incline.

Examples of reckless behaviour included riding two people to a car: the combined weight was too much for the brakes, and on one occasion the result was inevitable broken legs. A girlfriend riding on one's knee was a thrill in more ways than one! Daisy would have looked sweet upon the seat of a car gwyllt made for two.

In an attempt to limit the accidents the afternoon rush hour was led by a 'captain' whose job was to ensure a steady and smooth descent in an orderly fashion. 'But on occasions we would wait until they had gone and see how fast we could go,' said Emrys with a twinkle in his eye.

Children not yet teenagers would occasionally sneak into the works and take a car out in the evening. Sadly in the 1920s two of them were killed as they collided into a slate wagon.

The cars were private property, and each carried the initials of its quarryman owner. Some of them had detachable brake handles which would be removed to prevent them being taken by anyone else. Second-hand ceir gwylltion (plural of wild cars) would exchange hands when a worker retired or moved on. A new one could be ordered and bought for 10 shillings, and Emrys's father built his son's first one.

Emrys was unable to show me his first car gwyllt, but instead showed me the model made for the National Museum of Wales in 1925 – but it never made it to the museum. A lot of trouble and effort was taken in its construction, using local materials and skills with the wheel imported from the Porthmadog Foundry. When the museum staff called to collect it they were disappointed, they had wanted one that had been in regular use. The organiser reached into the nearby wagon and gave them someone else's, which in turn led to an uproar: he had no right to give away private property and the offer of 'new cars for old' was not appreciated.

The Craig Ddu quarry is thought to be the only place where ceir gwylltion were used.

Emrys explains the finer points of a Car Gwyllt

'The inclines were ideal,' said Emrys. 'Not too steep as to be impossibly dangerous, and without long flat stretches that would make it a waste of effort.'

The practice continued until the quarry closed in 1939, reopening for only a brief period towards the end of war to supply slate for repairing roofs bombed in the London blitz.

Having met Emrys and heard his description I walked up the inclines to imagine what it must have felt like as the four o'clock hooter was sounded and the men launched themselves down the mountain in their epic commute. Smoke was rising from the terraces of chimneys below and a sheep was watching me from where the rails used to be. Looking down to the coast and the sinking sun I couldn't help but think of the glamour and cliché of 'sliding into the sunset' a bit like cowboys.

Rock cannon

I've walked the footpath alongside the Ffestiniog Railway to Blaenau on countless occasions and each time is different, there's always something new to note or fresh to feel. It's a rugged landscape with derelict farm buildings and industrial heritage kept alive by the puffing and hooting of ancient steam trains.

When the railway was opened in 1836 the trains were powered by gravity, pony and water wheel – steam was not introduced until the 1860s. The brakes were released and gravity took the slate wagons down to the coast and ponies pulled them back to Blaenau. But for the first few years of the railway's life, just beyond the western end of Tanygrisiau reservoir, the wagons went uphill, one at a time, driven by waterwheel.

From the day the railway opened this short uphill section was a bottleneck, and work commenced on the first Moelwyn tunnel, the one that is now flooded by the reservoir. Six years later the tunnel was opened, and thereafter the train truly ran downhill all the way by gravity.

Just a few yards from the old section of uphill track there is a slab of rock surrounded by heather and wild grasses. A bit like any other slab of granite except this one has seventeen holes in it gouged 5 inches deep with a hand drill – I wonder how long that would take?

This was not a training ground for apprentice quarrymen, but a rock cannon to be fired on special occasions. The holes were part filled with black powder and covered with stemming (crushed stones) through which a goose quill filled with powder acted as a detonator. Connecting the various holes was a line of goose fat embedded with more black powder. Light the touch fuse, stand well back and enjoy the show.

Getting the right mix and balance of ingredients was vital – too little stemming and the explosions would be damp squibs. Conversely if the holes were too tightly packed with stemming the rock would be blasted to smithereens and this was the cause of many accidents.

This particular cannon is known to have been fired when the railway was first opened, and again in 1842 when the tunnel was completed, but it is just one of many. Throughout Gwynedd there are more than 250 such cannons that have been recorded.

The design of later cannons was refined with channels cut into the rock to link the holes together. Sometimes there are as many as 160 holes in a cannon. The timing of each explosion could be controlled or varied by the length of channel between the holes. In this way one of the cannons was designed to beat out the

Rock cannon to commemorate the opening of the Moelwyn Tunnel in 1842

(English) national anthem.

The greatest concentrations of cannons occur around quarries, especially those associated with the landed gentry: the reason being that they had a large number of VIP guests to impress, and what better way to do so than with a display of rock cannons.

Cannons would be fired to celebrate weddings, jubilees, declarations of peace, but probably the most extensive displays would be to welcome Royal visits. The Daily Mail's account of the Prince of Wales's visit to Blaenau in 1923 gives an idea of how impressive they must have been: '... each mountain sprang into eruption. The Prince sat in his car and crushed his cap into his hand. And while the roar of the explosions rose above the cheering he banged a fist into the palm of his hand and said, "I have never seen anything more wonderful – never".'

Special occasions such as weddings are best held on dry days – especially so if you're planning to fire cannons. On 6th August 1863 a Blaenau quarry owner F. S. Percival was to marry Miss Jones Parry and '... great was the rejoicing in the quarries as the day was a general holiday for them. A large number of rock cannon were prepared to be fired throughout the day of the marriage but that was prevented due to torrential rain.' The cannons were fired a month later on the couple's return from honeymoon.

The cannons have survived, albeit with plugs of moss and grass growing out of their holes, and whilst the practice of firing them has lapsed there is a group of local historians who have been experimenting and worked out the basic method. Walkers pass by without a second glance – imagine their surprise if magically one sprang into life! It would be great if we could get a couple of them into action again, maybe as percussion for an open-air concert with the BBC National Orchestra of Wales performing the *1812 Overture*!

Aberdwyryd – shifting sands

This beautiful estuary mouth is shaped by the action of 'long shore drift', a process whereby the sand is nudged northwards by the angled direction of the waves creating sandbars. Look on a map and you'll not find it as a place name but many stories can be told about the mouth of Afon Dwyryd.

The estuary is in constant flux with tides racing in and out revealing the routes of streams and the river flowing from the Vale of Ffestiniog. Across the waters to the north is Portmeirion, most remembered as the location for filming *The Prisoner*, with the huge bouncing balloon rolling over the sands.

In the middle of the estuary and slightly upstream, is Ynys Giftan sticking out defiantly. It's opposite the village of Talsarnau, which translates to 'head of the roads' and has been a major route for crossing the Dwyryd for thousands of years – one of the 'dwy rhyd' (two fords) that give the river its name.

Instead of paddling through shallow waters you could keep your feet dry by taking the ferry from the southern banks of the estuary to Ynys Cyngar above Porthmadog, which operated until the railway came in 1867 crossing the Dwyryd over Pont Briwat – Briwat is derived from Preifat, and that's why you pay a toll to cross it!

There was a small trackway along the southern tip of the estuary to reach isolated properties but in 1927 this was swept away by a massive tidal wave. A neighbour of mine, who lives a few miles inland at the Crochendy Maentwrog (Pottery), showed me the high water mark carved at waist height onto a slate pillar in his barn – a reminder of this Welsh tsunami.

The village of Ynys is aptly named, sitting like an island above the high tide mark surrounded by estuary, sea and the great marsh, but since 1806 the marsh has been drained with a network of ditches flowing out through locks into the estuary at low tide. If you look at the lock outside y Warws (the warehouse) and use your imagination it is easy to see that this was the route taken by boats to supply Harlech Castle. Forget the romantic vision of ocean going ships sailing to the foot of the castle: the goods arrived along y Gamlas, the canal.

After the marsh was drained a racecourse was established, y Ffridd Rasus, and this is where rich families such as the Oakeleys and the Vaughans would race their horses. The smooth surface of the nearby beach made a good venue for polo matches. Nowadays the site is used for much less glamorous purposes, being the landfill and recycling centre for the area.

The high point of Ynys is Llanfihangel y Traethau, the church of St Michael of the Beaches to differentiate it from all the other St Michael's – back in olden times

Michael (Mihangel) was as common as the Jones's. It is shrouded in yew trees and the walls of the graveyard are rounded, most probably reflecting pre-Christian use. In many cases the transition to Christianity built upon and adapted existing places of worship, making spiritual conversions more palatable.

Gravestones mark out the resting places for people with remarkable spirit. One of these is for Richard Hughes, the author of *High Wind in Jamaica,* first published in 1929. There is also a beautiful stained glass window presented by his children. Richard and his family had a long association with northern Wales and for many years lived at Môr Edrin, nowadays a holiday cottage looking north across the estuary and where Richard died in 1976.

Richard was a keen sailor and loved messing around with boats big and small. On one occasion he helped fit out a slate brig called the Rosetta and subsequently was a member of the six-man crew to sail it from Porthmadog to Belfast. The experience from this voyage feeds into the description of the pirate ship in *High Wind in Jamaica.*

Another gravestone is to the memory of Lord Harlech, who was a Cabinet Minister before becoming the British Ambassador to the United States, during which time he played a significant role in the Cuban Missile Crisis. He subsequently went on to be the founder of Harlech TV.

In a different league is Mary Evans (1735 -1789), known as Y Fantell Wen, White Mantle. Mary was the leader of a religious sect that wore white mantles on Sundays and held ceremonies on the mountains above Ffestiniog. She professed to be married to Christ and one of her assertions was that she would never die. As a consequence, when she did finally die, her body was kept 'in state' for a long time – but eventually she had to be buried and the sect died out not long after.

Up until the mid 1800s the estuary was a bustling freight route with two-man boats rowing slate downstream to meet waiting ships at Borth y Gest. There were about fifty boats and a hundred boatmen plying the waters, loading up at the several quays as far upstream as Maentwrog, going out with one tide and back on the next. Within fifteen years of the Ffestiniog Railway opening, the slate boats became a thing of the past, but an old one has been found pickled in the mud and is awaiting retrieval and restoration.

This idyllic peaceful location also has its memories of war. Tank traps and wire fences can still be made out as this flat stretch of coast was considered a likely landing point for an invasion from the west. There was a military camp based behind the dunes and Castell Deudraeth – now a five star hotel attached to Portmeirion – was the evacuation home for a girls boarding school.

Summer storms in 2007 rearranged the sands to reveal an American fighter plane that crashed in 1942. The plane was towing a target for the rest of the

Down the mouth of the Dwyryd towards Portmeirion

squadron to practice on, but the pilot failed to switch from the reserve to the main fuel supply, and the engines lost power. Landing in two feet of water he survived the crash but a few weeks later was 'lost in action' in a raid over north Africa. The plane, a Lockheed P-38 Lightning, has been nicknamed the Maid of Harlech and is incredibly well preserved with minimal corrosion. Within a few months of being revealed the sands moved again and once more the wreck is covered, protected from the elements and souvenir hunters, awaiting rescue for display in the RAF Museum.

My favourite way to approach the mouth of the estuary is in a *Chariots of Fire* slow motion run through the shallow waves, northwards along Harlech beach with dunes to the right, Snowdon ahead and Llŷn arcing towards Ireland. An uplifting setting full of stories about people and their struggles to survive.

War in the Vale of Ffestiniog

Most of us have lived our lives in peace and can only imagine what it must be like to live through war, but reminders are all around us. Even though the Vale of Ffestiniog was not in the front line it still has its stories to tell. Some say Plas Tan y Bwlch, now the National Park's Training Centre, was to be the Nazi headquarters in Wales, and that Plas Dôl y Moch was to be Hitler's local summer residence, but instead it's the outdoor education centre for Coventry City Council.

Driving out of Blaenau towards Betws-y-coed, up the steep pass called The Crimea, there's a strange memorial referred to as Tomen Esgidiau, the heap of shoes. It's nothing to do with the Crimean War which gave its name to the road that was being built at the same time.

A monumental mason has carved a headstone that reads Esgidiau Meirw, 'dead shoes', and placed it on top of the pile of military surplus boots. These were made or repaired at the improvised factory in Blaenau's old market hall. There must have been several lorry-loads dumped and burned here, but all that remains are the metal plates to reinforce the toe and heel of the sole, and the eyelets for the laces. It seems quite appropriate that this part of the national park is called Pedol Ffestiniog – Ffestiniog Horseshoe.

A slate memorial to the boots

At the outbreak of war Britain's precious treasures from the National Gallery needed a safe haven, beyond the reach of German bombing raids. As the prospects of war became inevitable, the works of art were transported by rail to be stored in Aberystwyth and Bangor and everyone breathed a sigh of relief when they were safely locked away. But with France being overrun so quickly, an even safer store was needed and quickly.

Bits of old military boots above Blaenau

Plans, supported by Lloyd George, were agreed to acquire and convert the underground quarry deep inside Manod Mawr, the elephant's head mountain to the south of Blaenau. False ceilings were erected to prevent damage from falling slate, endless racks were built to hang things from, and systems put in place to monitor and control humidity and temperature. After months of preparation the treasures were transported the final leg of their journey in containers on lorries. The road beneath the railway bridge at the base of the mountain was excavated to allow enough headroom for the lorries to pass, and all worked fine apart from one lorry which was slightly too tall and the tyres had to be deflated to get it through.

The staff of the National Gallery moved along with the contents, and the restorer set up his workshop inside the quarry. Lodgings were taken in nearby villages, whilst the director, Sir Kenneth Clark, took up residence at Portmeirion – not a bad place to oversee the Gallery from! By the time victory was declared the treasures had been returned to London, yet the refuge continued to be maintained and staffed by officials until 1982 when it was returned to the owners and slate production recommenced.

The area was also a safe haven for thousands of evacuees, and there is a great description in the book written by Richard Hughes' daughter about the 'six strange children' he brought home in the summer of 1939. They were part of a contingent of 800 children from Birkenhead that arrived at Penrhyndeudraeth station that day.

Penrhyndeudraeth is a real mouthful to English visitors but means the

111

promontory or peninsula between two beaches, those being the Dwyryd and the Glaslyn estuaries. Until the late 1990s this was home to Cooke's Explosives, and in its latter years the factory was owned by ICI. During the Second World War it employed more than seven hundred people. The site is divided into various sections and buildings so that an explosion in one part would not set off a chain reaction throughout the complex. Connecting the various areas was an underground railway, nowadays grilled off and a great roost for bats.

One man had the job of keeping an eye on the process of mixing the explosives, and to help him keep alert he was provided with a one-legged stool. If he did happen to fall asleep the consequent fall would soon wake him up!

Sadly there was a major accident on 14th June 1988, and the whole of the town shook as an estimated half a tonne of nitroglycerine exploded killing two of the workers. In recent years the site has become a nature reserve and is a good place to listen out for nightjars.

Coed y Bleiddiau is the name of the bungalow built by the Ffestiniog Railway in 1873 for Mr Ovington, the railway inspector at that time, and some people still refer to it as Tŷ Ovington. In 1937 it was let on a ten year lease to St John Philby, father of Kim Philby the infamous spy. At the outbreak of war his house guests included William Joyce, who travelled directly from Coed y Bleiddiau via London and thence to Berlin where he subsequently became the propaganda broadcaster Lord Haw-Haw, so named because of his toff's accent.

To add credibility to his propaganda he would intersperse the broadcasts with snippets of local knowledge and factual details. On one occasion he asked how the Johnson brothers from the Vale of Maentwrog were faring and how many had been injured in the futile war against Germany. Bob Johnson, one of the four brothers, went on to be the tenant at Coed y Bleiddiau for more than fifty years.

Lord Haw-Haw was captured and executed for treason at the end of the war in a case that went all the way to the House of Lords. The point of law in question was whether a foreigner (Joyce was an American citizen of Irish descent) could be guilty of treason (disloyalty to one's country) and the decision was yes! To this day the case survives as a legal precedent taught to all students of law.

Plas y Dduallt – the house on the black hillside

Perched high in the foothills of Moelwyn Bach with views across to the Rhinogydd and down the Dwyryd is an imposing house surrounded by the Maentwrog Nature Reserve with a private platform onto the Ffestiniog Railway. It's ancient and one of the oldest inhabited houses in Wales, dating back to the fifteenth century, and was home to the Llwyd family for more than three hundred years. As with many minor nobles they could trace their descent from Llywelyn Fawr and have left their marks on the house with attempts to carve Ll into oak window sills.

The core of the building is a hall house which would have been open from the slate slab floor through to the rafters. Today this is the dining hall, with a fireplace big enough to roast an ox in, and above it a magnificent oak truss bedroom with cruck beams joined by wooden pegs.

Most houses have a modern extension and this is no exception. Connected to

Plas y Dduallt - the house on the black hillside

the front of the original building there is another much taller house built in 1630.

It's just as well the Llwyds built the extension, as they soon received unexpected guests in the form of Cromwell's officers who were billeted here during the siege of Harlech (1647) whilst their troops were accommodated in the valley below. The cellar beneath the new house was also used to secure prisoners overnight on their way to the gaol at Ffestiniog.

The name of the house is Plas y Dduallt, a bit of a mouthful for novice Welsh speakers, but a name which translates simply to 'House on the Black Hillside'. The estate agent referred to some outcrops of black rock, but we've since been told the name alludes to things more sinister ... in days gone by people would do anything to avoid walking past the house after nightfall. What with Coed y Bleiddiau (Forest of the Wolves!) a few minutes away ... one's imagination can run riot.

As well as running their estate, rumour has it that the Llwyds of Dduallt went in for cattle rustling from the Drovers. There was also a trace of insanity running through the family, and the family tree in 'Griffith's Pedigrees' refers to several offspring with the single word 'idiot'. The Llwyds continued to own Dduallt until the mid nineteenth century, when according to a local chronicler, 'due to the habit the Welsh had, of excessive litigation, the family fell upon hard times'.

The house changed hands several times and 'suffered many improvements'. Instead of being a grand home for a powerful family, it became more of a farmhouse. The big rooms in the front house were partitioned and the two central windows at the front were swapped out for four smaller windows and a central doorway. The kitchen had collapsed and a makeshift kitchen was created in the dining hall.

The house was in decline, and during World War II became home to eighteen evacuees from Liverpool. They took up residence with few creature comforts ... no running water, no electricity ... but they did enjoy a swimming pool which can still be made out, a hollowed out section in the nearby stream. There's also a life-size sword carved into the bark of an oak tree, which is clearly visible sixty years on.

After the war the house fell into further decline, as did several other things in the Vale of Ffestiniog. The slate industry was in serious decline as builders switched to alternative roofing materials. The railway that brought the slate down from the mountains was no longer viable and the trains stopped running.

The house was empty apart from summertimes when it was used by the Reverend Hopkinson and his family from London for holidays. In those days there was no vehicle access to the house, not even for a tractor, so everything had to arrive by foot, by horse or along the railway line. The Hopkinsons used to load their gear on to a disused wagon at the next station and push it along the line. The wagon was once used in an emergency as an impromptu ambulance to get a

Snow on the line at Campbell's Platform

member of the family down the line to a real ambulance waiting at the next station.

In 1962 the Tan y Bwlch estate, which owned much of the valley including the village of Maentwrog, was auctioned off. Many tenant farmers became owners. The National Trust and the Forestry bought up some of the woodland and traditional grazing lands. And Colonel Campbell bought Dduallt.

As the name suggests he was not a Welshman but a Scotsman. Campbell served as an officer in the Black Watch, and was a qualified solicitor according to the jurisdiction of England and Wales. This meant that he was not able to practice law in Scotland, and retirement to northern Wales made a very good alternative, where he became the Solicitor for Meirionnydd.

The Colonel spent many years restoring Dduallt with assistance from the predecessors to CADW. The house had to be re-roofed, the kitchen re-built and the stone spiral staircase restored. The nineteenth century alterations to the front of the house were reversed. Windows which had been blocked off, presumably at the introduction of Window Tax in 1696, were uncovered with the original frames intact, complete with carvings such as the 'daisychain' to ward off evil spirits. Were it not for the Colonel and CADW, Plas y Dduallt would almost certainly be a pile of rubble by now. In 1976 the restored house was featured on the front cover of the Historic Buildings of Wales.

Whilst the house was going through a renaissance, so too was the railway line just above it with Colonel Campbell making a significant contribution. As well as the law, he had considerable expertise in explosives, and put this to good use in helping re-open and blast through the new line up to Blaenau. He also made the old farm buildings available for the volunteers (or 'deviationists', as they called themselves). Between 1965 and 1973 there were ten thousand bed nights … typically fourteen deviationists would be accommodated over a weekend in bunk-bed accommodation. Many relationships began here!

In return, the Colonel's epitaph is Campbell's Platform … a private platform from which the passing steam trains can be hailed by guests that stay here. During the Colonel's life he had a siding on the platform where he parked his own engine, and this he used as part of his daily commute to the office in Dolgellau, his car being parked a mile down the line at Tan y Bwlch station. The BBC made a classic documentary of the Colonel and his commute titled *The Campbells Came by Rail.*

Television cameras arrived again just recently, when we welcomed S4C and the Ty Cymreig team. Plas y Dduallt has survived five centuries of storms and outlived countless residents, and when asked how long we'd stay here, the reply was:

'*Dim ond y gofalwyr ydyn ni, ac yn y pendraw mi ddaw'n amser i'w basio ymlaen i'r bobl nesaf.*' ('We're only the caretakers, and eventually the time will come to hand over to the next people.')

Further information

Aran lamb
01678 540 603
For details on where to sample Aran lamb or to order produce from the farm at Llanuwchllyn, near Bala, call Maldwyn Thomas, or visit www.aran-lamb.co.uk

Bat Conservation Trust
020 7627 2629
For more information on bats, telephone, or visit www.bats.org.uk

Caffi Croesor
01766 770 456 / 07979 855 653
Croesor is the start and end of many great walks, but by car is best approached from the village of Llanfrothen, about five miles from Porthmadog. The Caffi is open five days a week, Wednesdays to Sundays, from 12.30pm until 5 or 6 pm, and will occasionally open on other days if the weather is fine and the car park full. Phone to check opening times.

Crûg Farm
01248 670 232
The nursery is about two miles outside Bangor on the road to Beddgelert, and is open from spring to autumn. For more details, including the downloadable plant list, have a look at www.crug-farm.co.uk

Hafod y Llan
01690 713 327
This wonderful farm is about two miles out of Beddgelert, on the way to Capel Curig. More information, including how to purchase organic meats, can be found at www.hafodyllan.org.uk

Maes y Neuadd
01766 780 200
Details about this great place, on the mountain road between Harlech and Talsarnau, can be found at www.neuadd.com

Plas Tan y Bwlch

01766 770 274

This is the stately home near Maentwrog (between Porthmadog and Trawsfynydd) which is now the training centre for the Snowdonia National Park. It is well worth getting a prospectus of their courses.

www.plastanybwlch.com

Plas y Dduallt

01766 590 272

If you'd like to stay in the cottage and hail passing steam trains from Campbell's Platform, more details can be found at www.snowdoniamanor.co.uk, or by calling us on the number above.

Rock cannons

If you would like to find out more about the history and location of Rock Cannons the book written by Griff Jones, entitled The Rock Cannon of Gwynedd, is an excellent read. It's not available from Amazon, but can be bought in local bookshops and at the reception of Plas Tan y Bwlch (see above).

Thanks to:

- Twm Elias and Andrew Weir, both from Plas Tan y Bwlch, for showing me some of the finest views of Snowdonia and sharing its stories.
- The late Merfyn Williams for impromptu lectures in the field, organised by Medrwn, the training organisation.
- Lynne, Leah and Nicky from Meirionnydd Oakwoods Habitat Management Project (now concluded), for inviting me to events in charcoal-making, hedge-laying, stone-walling, lichen and bryophytes, and building an otter holt. My social life will never be the same again.
- Kate Williamson, Rob Strachan and Chris Hall for teaching the difference between a mouse and a vole, and for getting me involved with Eryri Mammaliaid (Snowdon Mammal Group) I never knew how much fun it could be to spend a weekend scouring the countryside collecting samples of poo.
- Pauline Barber, Sarah Cartmel and the Gwynedd Bat Group for taking me into mines and midge-infested locations to count bats.
- Dr Rod Gritten, until recently the Senior Ecologist at the National Park, for taking me high up Snowdon to see the arctic alpines.
- Bryan Dickenson, for the finer points in conducting a goat census, and how to calculate the age of a goat.
- Wardens from the national park, including Jack Grasse, Rhys Jones, Arwel Morris and Bill Taylor, for explaining so much.
- Joze Mihelic from the Triglav National Park (Snowdonia's twin) for showing me what makes that corner of Slovenia so different from Snowdonia.
- The Meironnydd Running Club and the Blaenau Football Club for organising mountain races.
- The gardeners at Maes y Neuadd, for showing me what a proper kitchen garden should look and taste like.
- Glyn Davies, our local butcher in Penrhyndeudraeth, for introducing my family to the delights of saltmarsh lamb.
- Dudley Newbury, for teaching me how to cook a summer risotto with monkfish medallions and spicy salsa – my wife is even more grateful than me!
- Sue and Bleddyn Wynn Jones for taking me round their farm of exotic plants gathered from the far-flung corners of the world.
- Martha Newton, for explaining the difference between a moss and a liverwort.
- Tudur Owen and others in Croesor, for fighting for their community.
- Keith O'Brien and Trawsnewid, for breathing new life and hope into Trawsfynydd.

- Louise and Linda, for persistence in teaching me Cymraeg.
- Doug Oliver, from the Countryside Council for Wales, for explaining the habitat needs of the silver-studded blue.
- Allan Brandon, for introducing me to Odonata, and showing me the difference between a dragonfly and a damselfly.
- Arwyn Owen, Richard Neale and Trystan Edwards from the National Trust for taking me round Hafod y Llan.
- Dewi and Cynan, my neighbours, for letting me help gather the sheep and feed the cattle.
- Andy McAteer, from the Maentwrog Hydro Station, for keeping us 'green' and sustainable in the Vale of Ffestiniog.
- Keith Scrivens, the manager of the Mawddach Hatchery, and colleagues from the Environment Agency for helping save freshwater pearl mussels from extinction.
- The late Emrys Evans of Manod, for introducing me to the 'Car Gwyllt'.
- Griff Jones, for his excellent book on the *Rock Cannons of Gwynedd*.
- Myrddin ap Dafydd and Jen Llywelyn, of Gwasg Carreg Gwalch, for keeping me to the point in writing this book.
- Last, but not least, to my wife Sue for helping me to find time to write this book and for catching the magnificent seabass on page 75.